At Issue

| The Ethics of WikiLeaks

Other Books in the At Issue Series

At Issue

| The Ethics of WikiLeaks

Carrie Ann Taylor, Book Editor

GREENHAVEN
PUBLISHING

Published in 2018 by Greenhaven Publishing, LLC
353 3rd Avenue, Suite 255, New York, NY 10010

Cover image: Festa/Shutterstock.com

Cataloging-in-Publication Data

Names: Taylor, Carrie Ann, editor.
Title: The ethics of Wikileaks / edited by Carrie Ann Taylor.
Description: New York : Greenhaven Publishing, 2018. | Series: At issue |
Includes bibliographical references and index. | Audience: Grades 9-12.
Identifiers: LCCN ISBN 9781534502055 (library bound) | ISBN 9781534502116 (paperback)
Subjects: LCSH: WikiLeaks (Organization)--Juvenile literature. | Leaks
(Disclosure of information)--Political aspects--Juvenile literature.
Classification: LCC JF1525.W45 E84 2018 | DDC 025.06/3--dc23

Manufactured in the United States of America

Website: http://greenhavenpublishing.com

Contents

Introduction

On October 4, 2006, Julian Assange, founder of WikiLeaks, made the choice to release privileged documents signed by Sheikh Hassan Dahir Aweys that detail the decision to assassinate government officials. The following year, the so-called vigilante of digital data released the US Army manual for soldiers dealing with prisoners at Camp Delta, Guantánamo Bay.

Shortly thereafter, information about the Church of Scientology, the emails of US vice presidential candidate Sarah Palin, and a list of names and addresses of people WikiLeaks claimed belong to the far-right British National Party were made readily available to the public—without the express permission of the data owners. Future information breaches were often brutal, frequently embarrassing, and always controversial.

According to the organization's website, WikiLeaks specializes in the analysis and publication of large datasets of censored or otherwise restricted official materials involving war, spying, and corruption. The organization claims responsibility for more than ten million documents and associated analyses being made public through their actions.

WikiLeaks created a platform for the new age of civil disobedience known as "hacktivism." While Assange served as the initial face of this new endeavor, individuals like Edward Snowden, Aaron Swartz, and Chelsea Manning worked with Assange to challenge a long-standing status quo of who has the right to access details that influence the public's welfare. As a result, the stage of global protests evolved from the streets, public squares, and lunch counters to computer networks and online technologies, greatly expanding the avenues available for information sharing.

The continued release of information by WikiLeaks became the impetus for global discussions about censorship, ethics, government accountability, and the perceived sanctity of military secrecy. Connecting discussions was the overarching question of how all these issues balanced against the public's right to know the mechanics of how their world operates and insight into the true nature of their leaders intent and integrity. The public, the media, and the legal experts of numerous countries began to evaluate and question whether this disclosed knowledge causes irreparable damage to government relations, jeopardizes national peacekeepers, or risks simultaneously disclosing personal data unrelated to the conflict. Further, they began to ask what should be done if that knowledge was gained through illegal means.

Public debate continues in regards to WikiLeaks. To some, the people behind WikiLeaks are heroes who divulge information that sheds light on duplicitous policies of governments and corporations that negatively impact the public welfare, with WikiLeaks' ultimate goal being to hold oppressive regimes and negligent corporations accountable for their actions. To others, leakers are criminals, traitors, and detractors deserving of the harshest of espionage punishments. For most, there remains a struggle to define the legality and ethics related to the actions of WikiLeaks and the resulting consequences.

As more leaks occur and previously hidden information comes to light, the pendulum of public opinion swings. According to YouGov, research shows that public attitudes toward WikiLeaks are very different in 2016 as compared to 2010. Surveys conducted by the Pew Research Center in 2010 indicated that 60 percent of Americans who were aware of the release of US State Department cables thought this harmed the public interest.

However, by 2016, only 28 percent of those surveyed believed that the release of emails from John Podesta, campaign chairman of presidential hopeful Hilary Clinton, harmed the public interest. The shift is most pronounced among Republicans, 75 percent of whom say that the cable releases were harmful, while only 12 percent say that the email leak is harmful. Among Democrats, the change is minimal. Fifty-three percent who had heard of the cable leaks in

2010 thought it harmed the public interest, while 48 percent say that the email leak in 2016 harms the public interest.

Following the explosive release of leaks that included the Collateral Murder video (April 2010), the Afghanistan war logs (July 2010), the Iraq war logs (October 2010), and what became known as CableGate (November 2010), in a *Wall Street Journal* editorial (December 7, 2010), Chairman of the Senate Intelligence Committee Dianne Feinstein called for the prosecution of WikiLeaks and its founder.

She began her argument by stating, "When WikiLeaks founder Julian Assange released his latest document trove—more than 250,000 secret State Department cables—he intentionally harmed the U.S. government. The release of these documents damages our national interests and puts innocent lives at risk. He should be vigorously prosecuted for espionage."

Inconveniently for Feinstein and other US government officials, Assange is Australian and, as such, he owes no legal allegiance to the United States and is not subject to the Espionage Act of 1917. At the time of this printing, the investigation is ongoing and no formal criminal proceedings against Assange in regards to WikiLeaks have occurred. More than a decade after WikiLeak's first release of confidential data, its founder Julian Assange remains free of a criminal conviction, although he is exiled from the United States.

The same cannot be said for the many contributors of WikiLeaks. The espionage law and other information security policies do apply to US media journalists who put their freedom on the line in the pursuit of creating a transparent flow of information to the public to whom they are accountable. WikiLeaks has shown that security protocols are not keeping pace with the efforts of those who desire to openly disseminate information and, as a result, the twenty-first century will be marked as the age of the citizen journalist, the citizen watchdog, and the citizen adjudicator. Access to information by the public is greater than at any time before in human history, and the story of the ramifications of WikiLeaks is far from finished.

As the viewpoints in *At Issue: The Ethics of WikiLeaks* demonstrate, the questions of censorship, ethics, government accountability, corporate welfare, and the perceived sanctity of military secrecy remain globally contentious and, therefore, unresolved topics.

1

Citizens Are Defining the Age of Intervention

Paul Macmillan

Paul Macmillan has been a management consultant and strategic adviser to government leaders for over twenty-five years. Macmillan is the coauthor of the book The Solution Revolution *and frequently writes and speaks on topics of government innovation, public accountability, and advanced analytics.*

An explosion of mobile communications and social media is empowering citizens to define the next age of intervention and set new standards for public accountability. The light of transparency has never been brighter nor has the tolerance for misinformation ever been lower. It will be necessary for our culture to evolve so that the public becomes accountable. Now that citizens have the power to access and connect, it is they who can hold the government and corporations accountable.

The global financial crisis that began in 2007 has brought significant government intervention in developed countries worldwide. Financial system reforms, stimulus spending and direct capital infusions were just some of the initiatives deployed to stave off an even deeper recession. While these efforts have enjoyed some success, in many parts of the world the economic slowdown is far from over. Governments remain watchful over their economies.

Originally published in Paul Macmillan, "Government and the Publicly Accountable Enterprise: How Citizens Are Defining the Next Age of Intervention," *Deloitte Review* 9, July 1, 2011, https://dupress.deloitte.com/dup-us-en/deloitte-review/issue-9/government-and-the-publicly-accountableenterprise-citizen-intervention-in-a-connected-age.html.

Seeking to avoid another meltdown, they are working to rebalance the state of deregulation begun in the Thatcher-Reagan years.

While the level of economic stimulus and regulatory intervention was unprecedented, it has accompanied a more fundamental shift in the public landscape—one that may have further reaching and longer lasting implications for how businesses are governed and managed. An explosion of mobile communications and social media is empowering citizens to take hold of the public agenda. Mobile devices and social media are effectively ubiquitous—35 hours of video are being loaded onto YouTube every minute. In addition, social media have arrived as a legitimate source for news: According to a recent survey of more than 1,000 business journalists from over 35 countries, 90 percent source news from social media, far outstripping reliance on direct information from companies (21 percent) and analysts' research (13 percent).[1] While leading corporations understand the value of marketing through social media, the phenomenon comes with a price: The light of transparency has never been brighter nor has the tolerance for misinformation ever been lower.

With connectedness comes empowerment. WikiLeaks has received millions of documents from citizens eager to expose government and corporate secrets. As events in North Africa and the Middle East have shown, the political terrain can change rapidly when aided by the flow of news and information. But it is not just autocratic dictators that are impacted. Properly elected governments, global CEOs and iconic brands also face a new reality: Citizens are defining the next age of intervention and setting new standards for public accountability.

At the same time, citizen confidence in government and business has been shaken. Insider trading, Ponzi schemes, mortgage meltdowns, collapsing banks, product recalls and oil spills have convinced people that more active monitoring is needed. In response, legislation like Sarbanes-Oxley, and more recently the Dodd-Frank Wall Street Reform and Consumer Protection Act, have institutionalized corporate whistle-blowing. And while business and finance become more globally interconnected, the limits of national autonomy become more evident. The citizens of Iceland, Ireland, Greece and Portugal have come to appreciate how the demands and limitations of global financial markets can impact national economies.

Citizens are creating an atmosphere of transparency and accountability that goes well beyond traditional notions of corporate social responsibility. Boards of directors and executive management are under pressure to exercise broader accountability to the public. In matters of ethics and integrity, the line between shareholder and citizen expectations has all but disappeared. What justification, for example, would shareholders or citizens accept for doing business with corrupt dictators or with suppliers employing child labor? These issues now play out on a very public stage, with rapid consequences for marquee brands.

The Evolution of Intervention

Like many relationships, government, business and the economy have a long and sometimes stormy history. The creation of central banks to manage monetary policy; the establishment of crown agencies to provide critical infrastructure; the formation of the IMF, World Bank and European Union; and the introduction of regulated stock exchanges all indicate government's evolving role. In fact, there have been a number of distinct ages of intervention since the Great Depression.

The fault lines for the new age of public accountability can be traced to the beginning of the 21st century. The terrorist attacks of September 11, 2001 resulted in increased powers for governments to access personal information held by corporations. A series of well-publicized accounting scandals opened the door to governments strengthening corporate oversight. Defaulting financial institutions set governments on a path to define "too big to fail." Yet, perceived lax oversight of offshore drilling, widely criticized responses to natural catastrophes like Hurricane Katrina and the earthquake in Haiti, and a host of other challenges have cast governments, too, in an unfavorable light. Who is accountable when an offshore rig explodes? Or when financial products become so complex that neither traders nor regulators can understand them? In the past, a few investigative reporters would doggedly work to uncover the truth. Today, anyone with Internet access and a mobile phone has the potential to become a field reporter or government watchdog.

The Mainstreaming of Social Media

Social media have taken government and business scrutiny to a new level, with citizens mobilizing in ways previously unimagined by traditional government and business institutions. Sites like Facebook and Twitter have become a cultural phenomenon and let people organize and share information at a pace and scale never before seen. More significantly, they are a powerful tool for social change, giving the public the ability to build or destroy company reputations and influence government actions. On a single day, Saudi stock markets dropped 7 percent on fears that numerous "Facebook groups" were mobilizing protests across the region.[2] Social media's global reach and pervasiveness subject governments and businesses to unprecedented transparency and public accountability by spreading information faster to more people than was ever imaginable before.

These forces create a context for citizen intervention unlike anything we have seen. When WikiLeaks reported it was holding potentially damaging information on some of the largest banks, stock markets took note.[6] Given the media attention when information was released on diplomatic messages, it was not hard to imagine the reputational damage that the banks might suffer if such corporate records were released. Neither governments nor businesses can operate as they have in the past. Both are subject to global forces that are blurring the lines between private enterprise and public accountability.

In previous intervention ages, businesses needed to be concerned about their direct operations and maybe their impacts

Social Media on a Roll

- A 2010 study of CNN's international audience showed 43 percent of all online news sharing takes place through social media networks and tools.[3]
- Twitter membership grew by 1,882 percent from Feb 2008 to 2009[4] and in June 2010 reached 190 million visitors per month, generating 65 million tweets a day.[5]

on direct suppliers and customers. Today, the second, third and even fourth order consequences of their decisions are important, and these impacts can occur all over the globe.

The new age of intervention demands unparalleled public accountability. When the U.S. federal government introduced its massive $787 billion stimulus package with the 2009 American Recovery and Reinvestment Act, it recognized this and immediately set up Recovery.gov, a Web site dedicated to reporting on stimulus spending. The goal of the site was unparalleled transparency regarding where money was being spent and what was being achieved. In addition to project status information, including funding recipients, the site lets citizens report waste, fraud and abuse, mobilizing millions of potential citizen watchdogs.

Conventional business risks can be magnified by the potential for public intervention—whether by governments or citizens. Public risks can emerge without warning and rapidly go viral. Understanding and adapting to these risks requires an ability to see beyond the bottom line and to understand how citizens and governments may view corporate actions.

In previous intervention ages, businesses needed to be concerned about their direct operations and maybe their impacts on direct suppliers and customers. Today, the second, third and even fourth order consequences of their decisions are important, and these impacts can occur all over the globe. When poor labor practices of Foxconn Technology, Apple's China-based supplier of components for iPhones, came to light and then went viral, Apple recognized the scope of the problem and acted quickly. Reports that the suicide rates among the one million people working for Foxconn in China were similar to the national average added to the urgency of the situation. A third-party report into labor practices across its China supplier network allowed Apple to identify and acknowledge a number of problems, while outlining the corrective actions being taken.[7] The working conditions in Chinese plants would not have gone viral without cell phones and the Internet. Citizens on the ground are likely more vigilant watchdogs than any government inspectors—and they don't necessarily heed diplomacy or borders in utilizing the new tools of public accountability.

What the Future Holds

While the nature of government intervention tends to change with elections and watershed events, the implications of the age of public accountability are still evolving. But a number of trends seem highly probable, at least in the medium term.

First, governments will likely embrace a stronger regulatory role. This trend will probably be driven by stressed governmental budgets and a perception that businesses need to be held accountable.

The momentum of deregulation appears to have slowed, and governments seem poised to probably take a stronger role in everything from financial systems to environmental protection. With the ability of markets to self-correct or self-regulate in considerable question, governments will likely play an active role in managing global, national and—as seen in the case of energy production—even site-specific risks. Increasingly, instead of prescribing specific courses of action, governments are providing businesses with a set of expectations. This broader, outcome-based regulatory approach places increased responsibility on businesses to do the right thing in relation to both the intended and unintended consequences of their actions.

From a government agency perspective, austere times suggest that government agencies with the strongest economic, security, environmental protection and health-related mandates are likely to compete successfully for scarce government resources. Once funded, the agencies will likely face demands for increased transparency and a climate of public accountability, making it imperative that they show results by clearly enforcing compliance.

Second, greater public disclosure of corporate information will probably ensue. As privacy becomes a scarce commodity among citizens, there will likely be decreasing acceptance of walls thrown around corporate activities. Whether this scrutiny is "deserved" or "excessive" is a matter of politics and perspective, but the underlying reality is that more corporate information will likely become available to more people. In this scenario, the decision may not be one of how to lock down information so much as to how and when to present it, and in what venues. The recent decision by the U.S. Federal Reserve Board to release over 25,000 pages of documents showing which banks had used its discount window between 2007 and 2010 is an example of vaults of corporate information held by government agencies being unlocked.

Last, near-term agendas are expected to take precedence over big policy ideas. In the context of regulatory legislation, the methodical machinery of government has historically resulted in legislative and regulatory change only after extensive study. Governments, however, have become increasingly unlikely to spend years analyzing major policy changes. Cycle times have gone from years to months.

Nor do governments tend to rely on existing regulatory models to address new challenges. Citizens, special interest groups and politicians are coming to expect—and influence—more responsive policymaking. The good news is that feedback on government and business decisions is almost immediate. But it is challenging for a leader to persevere with a long-term plan when faced with short-term resistance. While this has led to more responsive government, it may well come at the expense of longer-term public policy solutions.

Navigating the New Public Landscape

Like most business transformations, a key to success will be cultural change, in this case with a particular focus on building a culture of public accountability. This involves encouraging staff to understand the publicly transparent environment in which business is conducted today and the speed at which reputations can be ruined and value eroded by poor decisions. Businesses need to be even more vigilant about what behaviors they want to be associated with, with responsibility for this vigilance recognized and shared throughout the organization.

There are specific actions that can improve a company's chances of successfully navigating the new public landscape.

Expand Your Understanding of Public Risk

Businesses need to expand their risk management responsibilities beyond regulatory compliance. Regulators, shareholders and citizens expect managers to promote public accountability throughout the enterprise and across the value chain. When Goldman Sachs was faced with political and public criticism in the aftermath of the subprime mortgage crisis, it established a Business Standards Committee to advise the board of directors with regard to the firm's products and services and how they were viewed by citizens. At an investor meeting, Chairman and CEO Lloyd Blankfein said that there had been a disconnect between how the company viewed itself and how citizens perceived it.[8]

Look at the Larger Public Picture

Boards and management must be mindful that repercussions of business actions can go beyond traditional business boundaries. By taking responsibility for a potential food contamination emergency and responding immediately, for example, a company may help maintain confidence in the broader public health system while identifying where corporate improvements might be needed. A company's decision to own the problem may prevent potentially counterproductive government action in a heated political climate.

Test Compliance Systems

Intense public scrutiny and a related demand for transparency are both on the rise. Consider worst-case scenario planning to stress-test not just corporate performance, but where broader public interests could be at risk. Contingency and disaster recovery plans should be updated to reflect the challenges of operating under increased public accountability. Obviously you don't want to do this by creating a crisis, but it can be simulated to create an instructive exercise.

It is important to stretch the boundaries in envisioning what a crisis might become in order to prepare. War gaming, for example, is a methodology that attempts to find and mitigate the weakest links in an organization. It is an organizationwide, pre-emptive, focused approach to test and validate how an organization will react to intense regulatory or public scrutiny. If a YouTube video is posted of an employee asleep on the job, how would you react? If four or five videos are posted on the same day of employees in different cities, what would you do? While a sleeping employee is (usually!) not a crisis, to an online media-addicted culture it can be an easily digestible mini-scandal.

Simulations can test the response plans of multiple agents within an organization as they react to pressure from regulators, consumers, politicians, investors and the media—all while complying with statutory obligations. Such testing can also uncover the strengths of the underlying and sometimes unstated assumptions and principles behind business strategies, revealing organizational biases that could undermine responsiveness to external pressures.

Collaborate with Policymakers

Governments are under intense public scrutiny to address increasingly complex challenges—assessing and managing system risks on a global scale and identifying and managing enterprises that are "too big to fail," for example. The scope and complexity of these and other risks will probably force business and government to collaborate intensively to meet public expectations and avoid catastrophic failures.

Governments make better decisions when they have a clear understanding of specific industries, issues and concerns. By moving from compliance to collaboration, directors can facilitate a dialogue between government and business that clarifies public issues for both. This is distinct from lobbying, which is often about advocating or influencing the specifics of a specific law or agency decision.

One way to enable this is for the board to include some members who have worked on the government side and therefore have an appreciation of how government agencies think and act. Without this competency, boards can fail to understand the complexity of government decision-making and how companies can best contribute to policy and regulatory processes.

Develop a Culture of Public Accountability
Across the Enterprise

Encourage executives and staff to think like citizens—rather than exclusively as shareholders or customers. Citizens are much more empowered today to hold businesses publicly accountable. What was once regarded as an acceptable corporate response to safety or other issues may not be today; and what's accepted today may not be tomorrow. Given the real risks of public outcry in the social media age, directors would be well served to monitor the pulse of core societal concerns to protect both the public interest and shareholder value.

At all levels of an organization, however, it is increasingly important for employees to understand and adapt to changing expectations on the part of governments and citizens. What are the potential implications of a particular course of action? If later called upon to explain our decisions, are we comfortable presenting our rationale to the public? Is there clarity within the organization as to how public accountability shapes our decisions? Among directors and management, there may be significant benefits realized in an environment where the potential public outcomes of business actions can be debated.

Citizens, as much or more than governments, are defining the new age of intervention. Empowered and connected, they are shaping a public agenda that holds business and government accountable like never before. Embracing this new age of public accountability is critical to navigating successfully in the future.

Endnotes

1. "Are analysts and investors engaging with new media?" http://www.brunswickgroup.com/insights-analysis/brunswick-review/brunswick-review-issue-2/research/engaging-with-new-media.aspx

2. Saudi Stocks slump nearly 7% http://www.marketwatch.com/story/saudi-stocks-slump-egyptian-exchange-stays-closed-2011-03-01

3. "Social Networks dominate online news distribution." Social Networking Watch. October 8, 2010. http://www.socialnetworkingwatch.com/2010/10/social-networks-dominate-online-news-distribution.html Web. November 18, 2010.

4. McGiboney, Michelle. "Twitter's tweet smell of success." Nielsen Online. March 18, 2009. http://blog.nielsen.com/nielsenwire/online_mobile/twitters-tweet-smell-of-success/ Web. November 23, 2010.

5. Schonfeld, Erik. "Costolo: Twitter now has 190 million users tweeting 65 million times a day." Techcrunch. June 8, 2010. http://techcrunch.com/2010/06/08/twitter-190-million-users/ Web. November 23, 2010.

6. Bank's stock declines on WikiLeaks anticipation. http://online.wsj.com/article/SB10001424052748703994904575647180698155858.html

7. Apple Supplier Responsibility 2011 Progress Report. http://www.apple.com/supplierresponsibility/

8. Goldman Sachs to create "Internal Business Committee". Huffington Post Business. May 2010. http://www.huffingtonpost.com/2010/05/07/goldman-sachs-to-create-i_n_567681.html Web. April 7, 2011.

2

WikiLeaks Has Violated the Security and Welfare of Ordinary Citizens

Jedidiah Bracy

As editor of Privacy Perspectives *and* Privacy Tech, *Jedidiah Bracy writes about the myriad views and developments that inform data security and information privacy. He also blogs about the intersections between technology, society, and privacy and writes feature articles for the Privacy Advisor and Privacy Tracker.*

WikiLeaks's rash and thoughtless actions have put the safety and welfare of the general public and national security at risk. While the organization's leaking of government documents can be seen by supporters as a boon to transparency, there is little to like about the fact that home addresses of Turkey's women voters were published, putting countless women in danger, or that sensitive personal information of donors to the Democratic Party in the United States is now available to the public. Exposing government or corporate corruption should not come at the cost of violating the privacy of public citizens.

WikiLeaks has been busy lately. Shortly after the failed coup attempt in Turkey, the controversial transparency organization posted around 300,000 emails of Turkish Prime Minister Recep Erdogan.

"Ethics and the Privacy Harms of WikiLeaks", by Jedidiah Bracy, International Association of Privacy Professionals, July 26, 2016. Originally appeared in *Privacy Perspectives*, a publication of the IAPP, at iapp.org. Reprinted by permission.

Then last Friday, Wikileaks posted nearly 20,000 emails and 8,000 attachments from high-level officials in the Democratic National Committee.

The latter, they proudly called part of their "Hillary Leaks series."

In response to the so-called "Erdogan emails," Turkey's internet governance agency blocked all access to WikiLeaks throughout the country. Many Westerners saw the national block as yet another case of government censorship of the highest order.

After last Friday's WikiLeaks DNC email dump, supporters of former presidential candidate Bernie Sanders angrily (and some would say rightly) pointed to the collusion amongst Democratic Party staffers that may have tilted the playing field against Sanders.

In both cases, WikiLeaks claims to be exposing widespread government corruption. And in both cases, in part at least, it's safe to say they are. But leave no doubt; both leaks are irresponsible, unethical, and parallel many of the issues privacy pros deal with almost daily. There's a reason, as of the writing of this post, Facebook has blocked all links to the DNC data dump.

Professor and social critic Zeynep Tufekci points out that the "Erdogan email" leak exposed "massive databases of ordinary people, including a special database of almost all adult women in Turkey." Indeed, the leak includes a spreadsheet of "what appears to be every female voter in 79 out of 81 provinces in Turkey," she writes. This includes their home addresses and, in some cases, their cellphone numbers.

Tufekci continues: "Their addresses are out there for every stalker, ex-partner, disapproving relative, or random crazy to peruse as they wish." This is also a country, she points out, in which hundreds of women are murdered and thousands go into hiding on an annual basis.

The "Erdogan emails" also contain sensitive data on AKP members (the ruling party in Turkey), including their full names, citizenship IDs, and cellphone numbers. This is significant because these are the same people who belong to a party that just faced a bloody coup; they could easily become future political targets.

In the U.S., the so-called DNC leak has already lead to the resignation of DNC Chairwoman Debbie Wasserman Schultz, long seen by Sanders supporters as a figure who prevented Sanders from getting the nomination over Hillary Clinton. It's also muddling up this week's DNC in Philadelphia.

Yet, like the Turkey email leak, WikiLeaks violated the privacy of countless innocent people in the process. The leak included 19,252 emails from some of the top brass of the Democratic Party. Some of those emails included personal information of donors, including credit card numbers, Social Security numbers, and even passport numbers. Plus, the leak needlessly exposed well-intentioned emails from politicians and professionals trying to do their job.

Just think about those professional emails you write to colleagues; you're not expecting the whole world will see them when you're writing them, right?

I understand that groups like WikiLeaks want to expose corruption and make corrupted official accountable, but does that good counteract the harm created by violating the privacy of thousands of other people—potentially exposing them to identity theft, embarrassment, or even physical harm? It doesn't appear that WikiLeaks has taken this collateral damage into consideration.

Why couldn't they redact sensitive information about innocent people?

In fact, with a total lack of irony as a so-called free speech organization, they're going after Tufekci on Twitter and threatening the Huffington Post with formal action.

The free press has traditionally been the institution to weigh such information flows and to work to do the most public good with the least possible harm. That's in part why NSA leaker Edward Snowden went to journalists Glenn Greenwald and Laura Poitras instead of publishing the entire trove of information he took with him from the NSA. He knew that publishing such information would have huge implications, and he knew they would wield such data responsibly. The media sifted through much of what Snowden shared, bounced ideas off government officials, got an idea of what may do too much damage to national security, and so forth.

They weighed the ethical and moral outcomes of what they were reporting.

This is a tradeoff and an ethical consideration many privacy professionals see and grapple with on a daily basis. Whether we're talking about creating expanded new personalized services for customers, A/B testing how end users interact with a social media feed, or sharing de-identified data with third parties or researchers. It's logical to argue there is an ethical foundation for the sharing of protected health information if it can help cure cancer, for example. We're talking about saving people's lives. But, even here, there should be privacy and security protections put in place.

On the other hand, companies rush to get a new product or service out, often at the peril of their users' privacy. Just look at the Gmail access issue that came out of the "Pokemon Go" craze. Millions of users unwittingly gave Niantic Labs full access to their Gmail accounts for a period of time. Even large companies face pressure to change with the times and experiment with their users' data. This is why companies need privacy pros. They need to help inform judgments that carry such moral and ethical weight. With technology further embedding itself into our daily lives, such judgements will carry huge benefits, huge risks, and huge implications for us all.

Clearly an organization such as WikiLeaks doesn't employ privacy professionals. But their actions demonstrate the careful attention organizations need to make when disclosing data. Information is more powerful in the Digital Age than ever. Those who wield that power must do so with great care and responsibility.

3

Whistleblowers Are Active Advocates for Change

Nozomi Hayase

Nozomi Hayase is a writer who has been covering issues of freedom of speech, transparency, and decentralized movements. Her work is featured in many publications.

Those in power can employ a tactic of concealing information, keeping the rest of us in the dark about what is going on. Julian Assange sees such manipulation as government conspiracy. Dissolving such a conspiracy by drawing the curtain on its inner workings is his mission. It is the responsibility of people with knowledge of wrongdoing to step forward to enact change, and WikiLeaks provides the information needed to enact those changes. The contagious courage of the whistleblowers—from Chelsea Manning to Edward Snowden—is helping to defeat the conspiracy of illegitimate governance.

In 2010, ongoing wars and government corruption spread through a fog of apathy. The world appeared to be reaching a tipping point for either global crisis or transformation. In this climate, WikiLeaks emerged into the limelight like a call to the conscience of humanity. Over the last few years, they released secret documents revealing Kenyan government corruption, Iceland's financial collapse, the criminality of US wars in the Middle East and more. Their very existence and what they revealed called

"WikiLeaks: Defeating The Conspiracy Of Governance," by Nozomi Hayase, PopularResistance.Org, January 3, 2014. Reprinted by permission.

into question the legitimacy of imperial power structures around the world.

Ever since its initial public insurrection, WikiLeaks kept making the headlines. In spite of founder Julian Assange being immobilized—first under house arrest and then confined in the Ecuadorian embassy in London—the stateless organization has continued to publish documents, shedding light on corruption and abuse of power. One might well have thought the life of this transparency advocacy group would be over after the massive US government retaliation and financial blockades by PayPal, Visa and other US financial giants. Yet, in the year 2013, WikiLeaks showed itself to be resilient and relevant as ever by releasing a secretive draft of the Trans-Pacific Partnership (TPP) treaty and aiding the world's most wanted whistle-blower, Edward Snowden, in his quest for asylum.

The inception of the WikiLeaks whistle-blowing website goes all the way back to late 2006. At that time, Assange wrote a kind of Manifesto called *Conspiracy as Governance*. In analyzing how corruption and secrecy are tied together, he described how "illegitimate governance is by definition conspiratorial—the product of functionaries working in collaborative secrecy ... to the detriment of a population."

In the introduction, Assange cited the words, "Conspiracy, Conspire" to mean "mak[ing] secret plans jointly to commit a harmful act; working together to bring about a particular result, typically to someone's detriment." The word "Conspire" originates in Latin; *con* (together) and *spire* (breathe). It means to breathe together. The common use of the word is by nature exclusive, where two or more people share the fetid intellectual air behind closed doors, shutting out fresh ideas and cleansing sunlight from outside. Conspiracy is sustained by inbred collusion of selfish interests. It is like smoke surrounding those who are bound by it, disconnecting them from the reality of everyday people who are kept outside of such elite circles and often exploited or harmed by their actions.

Assange saw how "a conspiracy … is the agent of deception and information restriction." Enactment of hidden motives of conspiracy depends on secrecy. Whether elected government officials or corporate executives, their interests are mostly divorced from ordinary people who are excluded from the circle. The primary motive behind this secrecy is to guard the self-interests of those involved.

The Battle Over Public Perception

Secrecy is created and maintained through two means. One is simply to close information off from access by the public through government classification of documents. The other is to deceive by way of "public relations"—propaganda used to control or distort public perception. Secrecy and corruption of government and the corporate state have reached a point of no return as the US government over-classifies information under the pretext of national security, including information that undeniably belongs in the public domain. "Currently the executive branch is the sole determinant of what is classified," activist and whistle-blower Sibel Edmonds said, pointing to how excessive government classification is being used as a tool to silence whistle-blowers.

Secrecy creates a gap in public perception and a loophole in the responsibility of governance. This gap gives power to rich corporations and governments to erase their bloody footsteps and hide the exploitative motives behind their actions. The power of secrecy is primarily the invisibility it grants to those actions who would be universally condemned if their actions were placed in the public eye. If the real motives and actual effects of rapacious forces in government and industry are kept invisible to those who are outside of the inbred circle, the conspirators can carry out their agendas without any real opposition.

Moreover, the Pentagon spends an ever-increasing amount of money on PR every year and there has been an alarming merger of commercial and government interests with mainstream journalism through the consolidation of corporate media. The forces behind state and corporate collusion are increasingly the primary forces shaping new laws and public policy—and these forces are heavily invested in maintaining control of public perception.

For instance, the actions of corporations overseas involving cheap labor and exploitation are largely kept out of public sight. This creates a gap between the actions of the powerful and how everyday people see the world. What people see are beautiful clothes displayed at shopping malls. The names on store tags such as Old Navy, Banana Republic and Gap found in the horrific aftermath of burned out or collapsed sweatshops in Bangladesh reveal this insidious practice, yet to the Western consumer it is just nice branding with appealing images of beautiful models. These kinds of corporations perform Orwell's doublespeak with ironic store names that carry colonial connotations as they manufacture consumer consent in their support of this exploitative model. Another example is the current round of negotiations over the TPP, which is a brazen attempt to subvert national law and individual enterprise so corporations can guarantee profits by overruling protections for the people and the free sharing of information.

This simple concealing of information and motives of those in power often goes hand in hand with the work of propaganda, keeping the public ignorant of what lurks behind the scenes. A vital part of PR work involves creating false perception regarding the merging self-interests of the elites; spinning a false image that those in conspiracy are working for the common good. This form of manipulation creates what the father of Public Relations, Edward Bernays, described as "an invisible government," which he observed as being the "true ruling power of our country."

Illegitimate Governance

We are surrounded by an invisible force of control. Assange saw through its inner working and pointed out how these governments that operate in secrecy are inherently conspiratorial and how such governance is by definition illegitimate. His observation led him to his first hypothesis for solving the problem of dissolving conspiracy.

He wrote that "when a regime's lines of internal communications are disrupted, the information flow among conspirators must dwindle, and that, as the flow approaches zero, the conspiracy dissolves."

Assange put this forward as kind of a mathematical formula that he thought could be used to dissolve conspiracy. Exposing secrecy = weakening trust lines of communication = collapse of conspiracy. With this act, the conspirators' power of invisibility from outsiders is undermined. In order for a formula to hold true and manifest, it needs a precise logic of architecture that would carry out each step. The act of becoming a watchdog on power usually comes from within the system, somewhere closer to the circle of conspiracy. This has traditionally come in the form of whistle-blowers. The original Whistleblower Protection Act (WPA) was enacted to ensure this necessary check and balance on power. Yet, recent years have seen a steady erosion of this law, and with Obama's aggressive prosecution of whistleblowers, there is no denying that this system of accountability has broken down.

The same can be said to some degree about the Freedom of Information Act (FOIA) that was passed by Congress in 1966, which set limits on government's withholding of documents. FOIA made federal agency documents except Congress and the Judiciary available to not only US citizens, but persons of any nationality upon request, with certain exemptions. Over the years, this has been rendered increasingly ineffective. One example is the case of a classified US military video of the incident on July 12, 2007 in New Baghdad, depicting three airstrikes from a US Apache helicopter (which WikiLeaks released with the title *Collateral Murder*). Reuters, whose journalists were killed in the video, tried to obtain the footage through FOI requests, but without success.

The Method of Leaking

It was in response to this breakdown of traditional checks and balance on power that WikiLeaks blazed onto the world stage with a new model of stateless free press that practices adversarial journalism. The method of leaking was made possible through a unique technical infrastructure. The system of anonymous drop-boxes provides a secure platform which helps those inside an organization have the confidence to step forward and reveal wrongdoing without fear of their identity being revealed.

Exposing secrecy can bring the actions of conspirators into the public eye and rectify distorted public perception. Assange described a particular kind of information that signals the presence of conspiratorial work. He explained how concealed information sends an economic signal for oppression because it shows someone putting economic input or work into concealing that information. This means it would be most effective to focus on the information that is most concealed and bring it out into the open, as that which is most heavily invested in keeping secret likely has the strongest effect when unveiled to the public eye.

Assange also spoke of censorship as a signal of corruption. He holds that censorship "reveals fear of reform. It means that the power position is so weak that [they] have got to care about what people think." After releasing authentic classified documents that are gained through an inside source, WikiLeaks disseminates this information as widely as possible with the intention "to get the maximum possible political impact."

In April 2013, WikiLeaks published a trove of 1.7 million US diplomatic and intelligence documents called *the Kissinger Cables,* spanning from 1973 and 1976. WikiLeaks spokesperson Kristinn Hrafnsson noted that hiding information behind the wall of complexity is also a form of secrecy. By developing a highly searchable database, WikiLeaks made documents usable that were normally quite difficult to access.

The Trans-Pacific Partnership Leaks

Then came the TPP leaks. On November 13, WikiLeaks released a complete draft of the Trans-Pacific Partnership's Intellectual Property Rights Chapter. TPP is a backroom corporate deal that enforces US interests and corporate hegemony over other countries. A major controversy over this bill is how its documents and dealings have been kept in extreme secrecy. Fast-track authority written into it is part of the corporate takeover of basic lawmaking, as only a few members of Congress have seen parts of it. Upon releasing the documents, WikiLeaks provided their interpretation in a short statement:

> If instituted, the TPP's IP regime would trample over individual rights and free expression, as well as ride roughshod over the intellectual and creative commons. If you read, write, publish, think, listen, dance, sing or invent; if you farm or consume food; if you're ill now or might one day be ill, the TPP has you in its crosshairs.

Critics call the bill "ACTA on steroids" and a "super-sized NAFTA," arguing that it violates privacy, sovereignty, internet freedom and effectively tramples many basic information and environmental protections. Its main elements undermine popular sovereignty and democracy and empower transnational corporations to change certain laws to suit their fancy. After WikiLeaks revealed this group of documents that seems designed mainly to expand US hegemony and corporate penetration, there was a serious backlash from civil rights groups and the other negotiating parties. Despite the Obama administration's aim to reach a deal by the new year, disagreements boiled over and the time-line for the agreement is now delayed.

Once concealed information is revealed, conspirators lose the cloak of invisibility and the public can grasp the tails of the conspirators' intentions. This begins a process that can lead to justice. In the case of the TPP leaks, people could see real corporate interests and agendas disguised as a governmental trade agreement. This is the formula: expose heavily guarded secrecy = correct public deception = bring about social and political transformation toward justice.

WikiLeaks' "mathematical" formula to dissolve conspiratorial governance seems to have begun proving its validity. Yet, as the world engages with deepening political and moral dilemmas, a more complex problem has surfaced within this increasingly corrupt and corporatized civil society. What new variable was added to the equation?

The Death of the Fourth Estate

There is no question that after WikiLeaks, the world had changed. The organization published documents evidencing war crimes and government corruption, but this is not all it revealed. Over the years, WikiLeaks has become the acid test that unveiled how the Fourth Estate has degraded into a conspiracy of consolidated corporate media networks. It is now more clear than ever how mainstream journalism has become a guardian of conspiratorial power rather than performing any real check and balance on corruption for the public good.

Back in 2010, former CIA analyst Ray McGovern, in an exclusive interview with Raw Story, declared that "the Fourth Estate is dead!" and described the US media's complicity with the Pentagon: "The Fourth Estate in this country has been captured by government and corporations, the military-industrial complex, the intelligence apparatus. Captive! So, there is no Fourth Estate."

Control of information and perception has become the real war of the 21st century. This year has seen the overreaching decay of the Fourth Estate as the ubiquitous Hollywood entertainment industry collaborated in character assassination. In contrast to powerful propaganda films about WikiLeaks, like the multi-million dollar DreamWorks film *The Fifth Estate* and Alex Gibney's *We Steal Secrets*, WikiLeaks themselves released a documentary called *Mediastan* to reveal the trend towards globalized media corruption, which also put forward their own narrative of these game-changing events that WikiLeaks helped set in motion.

In many ways, WikiLeaks embodies a new form of this essential function of the Fourth Estate. In a span of three years, they disclosed more relevant authentic documentation than all corporate news media combined. Yet in the process, they faced another conundrum. Anyone who strives for truth meets challenges, and Assange is no exception. In an interview with *Al*

Jazeera, he was asked by the interviewer what he expected and what he did not expect prior to the releases. He responded that after the release of two war logs he was surprised by the lack of public response to the leaked materials.

In a 2010 *Time* interview, Assange talked about the role of social media in assisting the work of WikiLeaks. He described how the analytical effort he expected from internet citizens around the world did not occur, so WikiLeaks, professional journalists and human rights activists had to do the bulk of the work. This relative lack of interest was also brought out during WikiLeaks *Operation Cablerun*, featured in their film *Mediastan*. The film followed a crew of WikiLeaks associates in a quest for media outlets to publish secret US diplomatic cables throughout Central Asia. One after another they met corruption, cynicism or apathy from publishers. With the undeniable global decay of the Fourth Estate, people's sense of justice and morality seem to have become neutered.

Martin Luther King Jr once said that "the greatest tragedy of this period of social transition was not the strident clamor of bad people, but the appalling silence of good people". What prevails today, after decades of corporate and state propaganda, is a passive and apathetic populace.

Re-Awakening the Civic Duty of Resistance

Leaking concealed information is fundamental for humane governance, yet without a dedicated public willing to check and balance the inevitable and increasing abuse of power, there is little possibility of effectively transforming corrupt structures and dissolving any conspiracy of illegitimate authority. The problem of our age takes a new twist. There is now another factor that needs to be added to the equation: the awakening of citizens who are motivated to perform civic duty to hold the powerful accountable and demand justice in a rapidly changing global landscape.

This leads to the deeper impulses behind leaking. In his 2006 paper, Assange laid out insights to dissolve conspiracy and stated how "we must use these insights to inspire within us and others a course of ennobling and effective action to replace the structures that lead to bad governance with something better." Assange clarified his insight on transparency, saying that "it is not our goal to achieve a more transparent society; it's our goal to achieve a more just society." Transparency through leaking is not a goal in itself, but a method for achieving an even higher moral goal. It is a way to break the shield of power that keeps citizens in the dark and to counter the kind of extractive and abusive behavior that human nature tends toward when working in secret.

Leaks are a way to break down walls, yet dissolving the conspiracy needs something more than simply releasing information. It requires an active force to confront and transform the centralized power necessary for those who conspire against the public good. Transparency in the form of whistle-blowing is a courageous act. It opens locked doors, bringing air into the deep reaches of a rotting system. It allows those close to or within it to breathe fresh air. What transformative variable arises when an individual decides to act on this principle of transparency that is crucial for dissolving conspiracy?

The Conscience of Chelsea Manning

In his formula for achieving fundamental change, Assange points to inspiration as a critical factor when combined with knowledge. It is indeed this inspiration from sources that is the fount of WikiLeaks's contagious courage. In an interview on *Democracy Now!* when he was asked what gives him hope, Assange responded:

> What keeps us going is our sources. These are the people, presumably, who are inside these organizations, who want change. They are both heroic figures taking much greater risks than I ever do, and they are pushing and showing that they want change in, in fact, an extremely effective way.

Now the equation advances: courage and conscience of the source + means of transparency = movement towards justice. In 2013, we have seen this contagious quotient of inspiration prove itself vital to the equation of dissolving conspiracy. Two weeks after the court-martial proceeding of Chelsea Manning began, an unauthorized audio recording of her initial courtroom statement spread through social media, despite the extraordinary secrecy surrounding her trial. For the first time after three years of silence, the world heard Manning's voice of conscience. In it, Manning laid out why she chose to release the massive trove of documents. After admitting that she was the source of the largest leak of classified information in history, Manning spoke about the motivation behind her actions:

> I believed that if the general public, especially the American public, had access to the information … this could spark a domestic debate on the role of the military and our foreign policy in general.

As she had hoped, her courage sparked new waves of insurgency. Manning's role in inspiring the Arab Spring was praised by Daniel Ellsberg, the former US military analyst and America's most renowned whistle-blower. On the first day of Manning's pretrial hearing, Ellsberg acknowledged her act as the impulse behind critical global movements that have quickly risen as tides of change for our time:

> The TIME Magazine cover gives … an anonymous protester as "Person of the Year," but it is possible to put a face and a name to that picture of "Person of the Year". And the American face I would put on that is Private [Chelsea] Bradley Manning… And, the combination of the WikiLeaks and [Chelsea] Manning exposures in Tunis and the exemplification of that by Mohamed Bouazizi led to the… non-violent protests.

In September of this year, Tunisian activist Sami Ben Gharbia paid homage to Manning for her role in inspiring the Arab Spring. He said the revolution "had to start somewhere, and the release of the cables started with Private Chelsea Manning, alone in the Iraqi desert":

> After she was sentenced to 35 years in prison, Chelsea Manning said in her statement that "Sometimes you have to pay a heavy price to live in a free society." I don't know if she knows that she helped us, in this part of the world, to move toward that

noble goal. Closing a cell door on a prisoner with a free mind has opened a thousand and one doors for a free society.

The Contagion of Courage

While Manning's act of conscience became a catalyst for the global uprising, it also paved the way for other whistle-blowers to courageously step forward. In 2013, the world saw a new wave of dissent. 28-year-old political activist Jeremy Hammond hacked into Stratfor, the Texas based global intelligence company to expose the inner workings of the insidious and pervasive surveillance state, including their spying activities on activists around the globe.

Right after his sentencing hearing this year, WikiLeaks finished publishing the *Global Intelligence Files*—over five million emails from Stratfor. In pleading guilty to one count of violating the Computer Fraud and Abuse Act (CFAA) for his role in hacking into the computers of this private intelligence firm, Hammond stated that "people have a right to know what governments and corporations are doing behind closed doors," and indicated clearly that he did what he believed was right.

At his sentencing hearing, Hammond spoke about how his act was inspired by his forerunner Chelsea Manning and her courage in exposing the atrocities committed by U.S. forces in Iraq and Afghanistan:

> She took an enormous personal risk to leak this information — believing that the public had a right to know and hoping that her disclosures would be a positive step to end these abuses … I had to ask myself, if Chelsea Manning fell into the abysmal nightmare of prison fighting for the truth, could I in good conscience do any less, if I was able? I thought the best way to demonstrate solidarity was to continue the work of exposing and confronting corruption.

Then came Edward Snowden, the former NSA contractor who blew the whistle on the most powerful surveillance entity in history. In a video interview with former *Guardian* journalist Glenn Greenwald, Snowden spoke of the motives behind his action:

I don't want to live in a world where there's no privacy and therefore no room for intellectual exploration and creativity…. My sole motive is to inform the public as to that which is done in their name and that which is done against them.

Snowden admired Manning and learned from his young forerunner. Behind the NSA leaks are others who were infected by their courage. Award-winning documentary filmmaker, Laura Poitras—who was the first media contact on the story—and Glenn Greenwald were both inspired by Chelsea Manning and Snowden's contagious courage.

In a statement he made one year after entering the Ecuadorian embassy, Assange called out the US government for framing those who speak truth to power as "traitors" and criminalizing them. He defended these whistle-blowers, describing them as "young, technically minded people from the generation that Barack Obama betrayed," and "the generation that grew up on the internet, and were shaped by it…" Assange then urged the public to help Snowden in his quest for asylum.

This past year we have seen WikiLeaks continue to walk their talk. When the US government revoked Snowden's passport, journalist Sarah Harrison of WikiLeaks helped him escape Hong Kong and inevitable jailtime in the United States. Months later, Snowden remains free to speak and engage in the public debate he unleashed.

"Citizens have to fight suppression of information on matters of vital public importance. To tell the truth is not a crime," Snowden wrote in his letter to the German government. On Christmas day, Britain's Channel 4 televised his message: "Privacy matters. Privacy is what allows us to determine who we are and who we want to be." In an interview with *Washington Post* reporter Barton Gellman, Snowden expressed his sense of victory and stated that his mission had already been accomplished. The genie was not going to be put back in the bottle. This contagion of courage cannot be stopped as people have begun to inspire each other.

The Courage to Inspire

Snowden's pursuit for asylum has created a new discourse. WikiLeaks journalist Sarah Harrison played a crucial role in making this possible. Referring specifically to Chelsea Manning, who is now serving decades behind bars, Harrison explained the reason for risking her life and liberty to accompany Snowden thus: "there needs to be another narrative … There needs to be a happy ending. People need to see that you can do this and be safe." In her November 6 statement, Harrison articulated her conviction of the importance for transparency that was demonstrated in her extraordinary commitment to source protection:

> When whistle-blowers come forward, we need to fight for them so others will be encouraged. When they are gagged, we must be their voice. When they are hunted, we must be their shield. When they are locked away, we must free them. Giving us the truth is not a crime. This is our data, our information, our history. We must fight to own it.

The 30th *Chaos Communication Congress (CCC)* held in Hamburg in the last days of 2013 saw a significant increase in the number of participants, which showed how this whistle-blower support community is thriving. In the opening keynote speech, Glenn Greenwald shared with the audience the profound impact Snowden's act had on him and on people around the world:

> The courage and the principled act of conscience that he displayed will shape and inspire me for the rest of my life, and will inspire and convince millions and millions of people to take all sorts of acts that they might not have taken because they've seen what good for the world can be done by even a single individual.

Later he reminded the crowd of Harrison's heroic act as well. Greenwald empowered the audience, noting that there is now a huge network of human beings around the world who believe in causes for transparency and who devote time and sacrifice for it.

Assange joined the CCC talk "Sysadmins of the World, Unite!" via Skype with Jacob Applebaum, independent journalist and security expert, and with Harrison, who was welcomed with a standing ovation by more than 4.000 people. Assange spoke to the audience about how high-tech workers compose a particular class and how, as system administrators, they are part of an important administration of interconnected individual systems. He encouraged these administrators to unite in their fight for internet freedom, reminding them how they "have extraordinary power, in a way that is really an order of magnitude different to the power industrial workers had back in the 20th century."

Applebaum asked the audience "what is it that you feel like you can do?" and emphasized the positive contribution one can make, each in their own way. He used Harrison's action as an example that embodies individual courage and creates a link that inspires others.

Inspiration is an antidote to conspiracy. It is like a compassionate bullet that brings down the walls around armored hearts and breaks up the conspiring of narrow interests. In solving the problem of illegitimate governance, we are now waking up to the fact that ordinary people are the vital quantity for the equation. The numbers are growing as the new network of awakened and impassioned individuals expands.

Activist Gregg Housh pointed to the decline of true investigative journalism and noted how the failure of the press in holding the government accountable has created a vacuum. He noted how "that void grew for years, and finally when we could stand it no more it got filled … by Anonymous, WikiLeaks, new whistle-blowers, and a new prevalent culture of transparency."

On November 15, Jeremy Hammond was sentenced to 10 years in prison and three years of supervised release at the Federal District Court for the Southern District of New York. As he was escorted out of the courtroom, to the crowd of supporters, Hammond pumped a fist in the air and said "Long live Anonymous!"

Online and off, the trend of civil disobedience refuses to go away. In response to the brutal indiscriminate shelling of Gaza in November 2012 by the Israel Defense Forces (IDF), Anonymous engaged in DDoS attacks and took down hundreds of Israeli websites. On November 5th 2013, protesters wearing Anonymous Guy Fawkes masks gathered all around the world to rally in over 400 cities for the Million Mask March.

In her impassioned speech after Hammond's sentencing Bria Grace of JeremyHammond.net spoke of how Hammond "is the reason a flame has been lit in so many of us." The torch of justice is carried through his courageous acts, and its light burns ever stronger.

Three years after WikiLeaks came to public prominence, where are we with the equation in Assange's *Conspiracy as Governance*? Has it been tested and its solution enacted? As leaked documents continue to shed light on the darkness of the world, illegal wars, drone attacks, bankster heists and corporate dirty deals continue. Yet thanks to Manning, we now have a clearer picture what modern war really looks like and the extent to which the military-industrial complex has morally bankruptcy itself. Thanks to Hammond, we are more aware of the collusion of governments and corporations in a network of spying on activists. Thanks to Snowden's NSA files, we are now only beginning to see the latent tyranny of an out-of-control surveillance state.

2013 was the year that we saw the courage of individuals who speak truth to power become truly contagious. There is no doubt that in this past year, WikiLeaks and other budding organizations have helped the world move one step closer toward a more humane form of self-governance. More and more people are counting themselves into the equation. In the presence of love, hatred cannot last. In the light of transparency darkness dissolves, and in the presence of inspiration people can no longer conspire. Each person's act of conscience breathes into the other, eventually becoming the critical mass needed to solve the critical moral math of our time.

4

Human Rights Through Nonviolent Means

Stuart Rees

Stuart Rees is an Australian academic, author, and human rights activist. He founded the Sydney Peace Foundation and is an emeritus professor at the Center for Peace and Conflict Studies at the University of Sydney in Australia. In 2005, he was awarded the Order of Australia for services to international relations.

In a controversial move, the Sydney Peace Foundation awarded Julian Assange its gold medal for the pursuit of human rights. While some may see Assange's work as diabolical and irresponsible, the Sydney Peace Foundation felt Assange's mission was in line with its values. Significant contributions to society are rarely free of conflict. Assange's actions provide a more important service. The public has the right to know how they are being governed so they can make informed choices about their leadership, and WikiLeaks plays a critical role in helping keep the public informed.

In a ceremony at London's Frontline Club on Tuesday, May 10, before an array of television crews from around the world, WikiLeaks co-founder Julian Assange received the Sydney Peace Foundation's gold medal "for extraordinary courage in pursuit of universal human rights."

In presenting the award, the former chair of the Foundation, the highly esteemed television journalist Mary Kostakidis,

"Stuart Rees in The Conversation: Peace Medal to Wikileaks Founder Was Controversial, but Warranted", by Professor Stuart Rees, Sydney Peace Foundation, May 18, 2011. Reprinted by permission.

congratulated Julian Assange on his courageous advocacy of people's right to know about decisions being made in their name by powerful political, business and military leaders.

Mary commented that the WikiLeaks release of hundreds of thousands of diplomatic cables had not only informed the public but in so doing had made a significant contribution to social justice.

As Director of the Foundation, I explained that although our major responsibility is to award annually Australia's only international prize for peace, it does occasionally—four times in the past fourteen years—award this peace medal for initiatives which make a difference to people's understanding of peace with justice and the means of achieving such a goal.

The distinction between peace—an end to violence—and peace with justice—the struggle for human rights through non violent means—explains the Foundation's rationale for making this exceptional and unusual award to Julian Assange.

I acknowledged that although this Australian citizen may be controversial and in some people's eyes so is the Foundation's decision to present him with an award, nevertheless it is the case that those who contribute significantly to justice will always be involved in conflict and controversy.

The alternative is to adopt a cautious consensus approach to governance and thereby disturb nothing and no-one.

Contributor to Democracy

The Foundation regards Assange and his WikiLeaks organisation as contributing to democracy, assuming that the operation of democracy includes the task of holding powerful people and institutions accountable, promoting freedom of information and, in the administration of justice, insisting on each citizen's presumption of innocence.

Over the centuries, the leaders of governments of many kinds have considered secrecy to be an efficient way to conduct business, but in 1790 in The Rights of Man, Tom Paine wrote that the case for secrecy was only justified by leaders who considered the skills of governing so mysterious that only they could and should know about them.

Luckily for the cause of greater transparency in government and for those who promote human rights, a company of dissenters, from Tom Paine to Daniel Ellsberg of Pentagon Papers fame, from Independent Australian MP Andrew Wilkie to Julian Assange, have revealed the dangers to the public if decisions remain secret and if decision makers are not held accountable.

Shameful Response

The Sydney Peace Foundation was also motivated to reward this Australian citizen because it was ashamed of the initial cowardly response of the Australian government when the Prime Minister behaved as though Assange had committed an offence and would not be welcome in this country.

That misreading of events was compounded by Attorney General Robert McClelland who claimed that Assange should perhaps have his passport confiscated.

It sounded as though the Australian Government was once again dancing to the US government's tune.

A Challenge to the US Position

The Peace Foundation also wanted to challenge the violent response of American politicians and media commentators.

For example, US Vice President Joe Biden said that WikiLeaks should be identified as an international terrorist organisation and presidential hopeful, Sara Palin wanted Julian Asssange "hunted down like bin Laden".

At the London ceremony I criticised the US Government's "bestial treatment" of the alleged whistle blower Bradley Manning who, until recent protests from civil rights groups, was reportedly held naked in solitary confinement for 23 hours a day.

Such conduct by government flows from that culture of revenge which influences politicians and their media supporters into thinking that extreme forms of punishment and humiliation will teach people a lesson.

It never has. It never will. Julian Assange, Bradley Manning and their supporters have repudiated such a culture.

Tributes

The final tributes to Julian Assange came from two great human rights campaigners, one who wrote his tribute only a couple of days before the London ceremony and the other, with crystal ball in hand, wrote his tribute over three hundred years ago.

Writing from Boston, Massachusetts, Professor Noam Chomsky sent the following message to Julian: "I would like to thank you for fulfilling your responsibilities as a member of free societies whose citizens have every right to know what their government is doing."

The other tribute came from Daniel Defoe, the author of such famous novels as Moll Flanders and Robinson Crusoe.

Defoe was also a pamphleteer and satirist who challenged the conformity of his day—a close alliance between church and state—and for such challenge was sentenced to time in Newgate prison and in the pillory.

While in prison he wrote the long satirical poem *Hymn To The Pillory* in which he hailed the values of free speech and demanded an end to the authoritarianism which prevented citizens from exercising freedom and experiencing liberty.

Four lines from that poem provided the cue for Mary Kostakidis to ask Julian Assange to accept the Sydney Peace Foundation's gold medal.

Defoe wrote:

Exhort the justice of the land
Who punish what they will not understand,
Tell them he stands exalted there
For speaking what they would not hear.

5

The US Government's Condemnation of WikiLeaks Is Ironic

Nicole Colson

Nicole Colson is a reporter for Socialist Worker *and a contributor to the* International Socialist Review *and* CounterPunch. *She frequently writes on civil liberties, the environment, women's rights, and culture.*

The reactions of US government officials to WikiLeaks have ranged from calls for deep investigation all the way to Julian Assange's murder. Why do those who believe in a democratic government like that of the United States have such strong reactions to making information transparent? Attempts by the government and some journalists to smear Julian Assange seem to go against the principle of freedom of speech. Suppressing WikiLeaks is exactly how the government maintains the status quo, and there is a moral imperative to disrupt these practices.

U.S. Politicians are baying for the blood of Julian Assange, head of the muckraking Web site WikiLeaks.

The latest release from WikiLeaks—this time consisting primarily of some 250,000 leaked U.S. diplomatic cables, about half of which are classified, either at the "confidential" or "secret" level—has politicians and pundits demanding that the Web site be shut down and Assange immediately jailed...or worse.

WikiWitchhunt," by Nicole Colson, International Socialist Organization, December 6, 2010. Reprinted by permission.

Reaction from Republicans was the loudest, of course. Rep. Peter King of New York called for Assange to be jailed under the Espionage Act and asked whether WikiLeaks could be designated a "terrorist organization"—a move that would make anyone working or contributing to the site vulnerable to prosecution by the U.S. government.

Senate Republican leader Mitch McConnell called Assange "a high-tech terrorist" on NBC's *Meet The Press* and said that if it's found that Assange hasn't actually violated the law by releasing the cables, then the law should be changed to allow retroactive prosecution.

Then, of course, there are the politicians who think Assange and anyone else associated with WikiLeaks should be assassinated. Former presidential candidate Mike Huckabee said that the person who leaked the information to Assange should be tried for treason and executed. Conservative *Weekly Standard* editor and Fox News contributor William Kristol stated that he believes that the CIA should "neutralize" the WikiLeaks founder.

Former Alaska Gov. Sarah Palin, meanwhile, took to Facebook to proclaim that Assange is an "anti-American operative with blood on his hands."

Assange is not a journalist "any more than the 'editor' of al-Qaeda's new English-language magazine *Inspire* is a 'journalist,'" claimed Palin. "His past posting of classified documents revealed the identity of more than 100 Afghan sources to the Taliban. Why was he not pursued with the same urgency we pursue al-Qaeda and Taliban leaders?" Palin said.

Jeffrey Kuhner of the *Washington Times* went even further. In an article titled "Assassinate Assange," he wrote that "Julian Assange poses a clear and present danger to American national security. The WikiLeaks founder is more than a reckless provocateur. He is aiding and abetting terrorists in their war against America. The administration must take care of the problem—effectively and permanently." The piece was accompanied with a mock poster of

Assange—with a target and bloody splotches over it and the words "Wanted Dead or Alive."

Fox News' Bill O'Reilly allowed that Assange should have the benefit of a trial—but that he should be executed when it's over.

For it's part, the Obama administration avoided explicit calls for Assange to be murdered. But it's clear that the administration would jail him, at the very least, if it gets the shot.

Attorney General Eric Holder announced an investigation into any criminal wrongdoing by WikiLeaks, warning, "This is not saber-rattling." Calling the WikiLeaks probe "an active, ongoing criminal investigation," Holder told reporters: "To the extent that we can find anybody who was involved in the breaking of American law, who put at risk the assets and the people I have described, they will be held responsible; they will be held accountable."

Obama's White House has reportedly barred all "unauthorized" government employees from viewing WikiLeaks. Likewise, the Pentagon has ordered the branches of the U.S. military to tell service members that the site is off-limits for both public and personal usage.

The attitude of Washington appears to be that it can limit the damage from this latest WikiLeaks release and "put the genie back in the bottle," so to speak, by sending Secretary of State Hillary Clinton into "damage control mode" to smooth over the ruffled feathers of U.S. allies, while going after WikiLeaks and Assange to prevent any future leaks.

Democratic Sen. Dianne Feinstein, who chairs the Senate Intelligence Committee, announced that she supports rewriting and expanding the Espionage Act of 1917 to make it easier to prosecute WikiLeaks. Sen. Joe Lieberman, chair of the Senate Homeland Security Committee, has been particularly aggressive, alternately threatening and cajoling various U.S. Web service providers and other companies into cutting off WikiLeaks.

Amazon.com was first to stop hosting the site, reportedly less than 24 hours after being contacted by Lieberman's staff. According to Talking Points Memo, Lieberman's staff "called Amazon to ask about it, and left questions with a press secretary, including, 'Are there plans to take the site down?'" Soon after, Amazon booted WikiLeaks for "unspecified" violations of the company's terms of use.

As Lieberman's spokeswoman Leslie Phillips told reporters, "Sen. Lieberman hopes that the Amazon case will send the message to other companies that might host WikiLeaks that it would be irresponsible to host the site."

Mission accomplished.

After Amazon caved, Seattle-based software company, Tableau, removed charts uploaded by WikiLeaks, according to the *New York Times*, "in response to Sen. Joe Lieberman's public statement that companies should stop helping the whistle-blowers." This is despite the fact that the charts only summarized the material—counting the number of documents per country, etc—and didn't provide any details of the leaked memos beyond generalities.

WikiLeaks' domain-name service provider, EveryDNS, was also battered by denial of service attacks, and the Internet payment site PayPal has since frozen the account of the German foundation accepting donations for WikiLeaks. (The static IP address for the site remains accessible.)

As Wired.com noted, PayPal froze the account because of supposed "illegal activity":

> PayPal's public statement doesn't detail the "illegal activity" WikiLeaks promotes, but presumably, it's the leaking of classified information. Sometimes such leaks are indeed illegal. And sometimes classified leaks—legal or not—reveal warrantless wiretapping of Americans, secret CIA prison networks and massive government waste hidden in black budgets. The reasoning PayPal offers for its newfound intolerance for WikiLeaks would seem to apply equally well to the *New York Times* and the *Washington Post*.

The irony about the push by U.S. officials to close down WikiLeaks, of course, is that the U.S. establishment is highly critical of governments like Iran's and China's when they attempt to censor the Internet. As the *Washington Post* put it, "Authoritarian governments and tightly controlled media in China and across the Arab Middle East have suppressed virtually all mention of the documents, avoiding the public backlash that could result from such candid portrayals of their leaders' views."

But when it's the U.S. attempting to do the censoring and keep official secrets away from the public, suddenly a little "authoritarianism" doesn't seem so bad. In fact, few in the mainstream media have called out U.S. political figures for their attempts to censor the documents and prevent information about the reality of the wars in Afghanistan and Iraq, not to mention the ugly truth of world "diplomacy," from reaching the public.

As Salon.com's Glenn Greenwald noted:

> Note that Lieberman here is desperate to prevent American citizens—not The Terrorists—from reading the WikiLeaks documents which shed light on what the U.S. government is doing. His concern is domestic consumption. By his own account, he did this to "send a message to other companies that might host WikiLeaks" not to do so. No matter what you think of WikiLeaks, they have never been charged with, let alone convicted of, any crime; Lieberman literally wants to dictate— unilaterally—what you can and cannot read on the Internet, to prevent Americans from accessing documents that much of the rest of the world is freely reading.
>
> The Internet, of course, is rendering decrepit would-be petty tyrants like Lieberman impotent and obsolete: WikiLeaks moved its website to a Swedish server and was accessible again within hours. But any attempt by political officials to start blocking Americans' access to political content on the Internet ought to provoke serious uproar and unrest.

Aside from facing calls for his assassination from various media personalities and politicians, Julian Assange is now a wanted man based on allegations that seem suspect, to say the least.

Interpol recently issued a "red notice" announcing that Assange is wanted for questioning over sexual assault charges in Sweden, and in a statement given to NBC News, the Swedish Prosecution

Office said Assange had been "detained in his absence, charged with rape, sexual molestation and illegal coercion." A Swedish court has refused to allow Assange to appeal against an arrest warrant.

While details of the allegations remain sketchy—a variety of reports indicate the accusations against Assange fall far short of rape—one matter that is certain is that Interpol's issuing of a red notice—which is typically reserved for violent criminals, international drug lords and war lords—for Assange is wild overreach. Rape is a serious allegation that ought to be investigated—but it's impossible to take the charges against Assange at face value given the nature of the attack on him by the world's superpowers.

Instead, it seems likely that the Swedish charges, as well as the Interpol notice, are designed to get the Australian-born Assange into custody in a country that will, eventually, be willing to extradite him to the U.S. to face prosecution for whatever "crimes" American prosecutors can conjure up around the WikiLeaks revelations.

But the international manhunt for Assange and the American media's guilty-until-proven-innocent attitude is in stark contrast to the lack of outrage about the governments and military officials that WikiLeaks has again proved are guilty of enabling murder, massacres and torture.

It isn't even that the latest WikiLeaks revelations are so shocking. Compared to earlier WikiLeaks exposés of U.S. troops engaging in war crimes, undisclosed civilian casualties, and complicity in torture in Iraq and Afghanistan, the cables showing that U.S. diplomats compared Russian Prime Minister Vladimir Putin and President Dmitri Medvedev to Batman and Robin are pretty mild.

Beyond the diplomatic name-calling, of course, there *are* important revelations in the new documents—including the fact that the Obama administration pressured the Spanish government to drop a criminal probe into Bush administration officials' complicity in torture, and that the head of the Bank of England got caught pressuring Conservative Party politicians to carry out harsher austerity measures, in violation of his job.

But even the most damaging WikiLeaks revelations are not very surprising. It has always been the case that behind the mask of "diplomacy" and fine-sounding rhetoric, there exists a snarling band of cynical politicians, willing to go to any expense to preserve U.S. dominance.

The reason the chorus of official fury over WikiLeaks is so loud is that WikiLeaks is continuing to expose the real aims at the heart of U.S. wars—a desire for power and conquest, and a willingness to run roughshod over human rights to accomplish them.

Each WikiLeaks "dump" of documents has produced a standard response from government officials. First come claims that the release of information is a threat to national security, then the contradictory assertion that "there's nothing new to see." And much of the U.S. mainstream media repeats both lines, interchangeably, ad nauseum.

Focusing on Julian Assange and the supposed "threat" he poses is far easier for politicians and the media than dealing with the disclosures of U.S. complicity in massacres and torture. As Glenn Greenwald noted:

[W]e're supposed to have an open government—a democracy—everything the government does is presumptively public, and can be legitimately concealed only with compelling justifications. That's not just some lofty, abstract theory; it's central to having anything resembling "consent of the governed."

But we have completely abandoned that principle; we've reversed it. Now, everything the government does is presumptively secret; only the most ceremonial and empty gestures are made public. That abuse of secrecy powers is vast, deliberate, pervasive, dangerous and destructive. That's the abuse that WikiLeaks is devoted to destroying, and which its harshest critics—whether intended or not—are helping to preserve.

There are people who eagerly want that secrecy regime to continue: namely, (a) Washington politicians, permanent state functionaries and media figures whose status, power and sense of self-importance are established by their access and devotion to that world of secrecy, and (b) those who actually believe that—

despite (or because of) all the above acts—the U.S. government somehow uses this extreme secrecy for the good.

The latest word is that Assange and WikiLeaks are planning to release documents from a major U.S. bank next—possibly Bank of America. We can only hope WikiLeaks gives giant corporations the same black eye it's given to the U.S. government—and we continue to defend its right to do so.

6

Changing the Free Speech Movement

Monica Morrill

Monica Morrill is a geographer who focuses on government economics, regulation, and policies. She is a contributor to SFPPR News & Analysis, *an online publication of the Washington-based Selous Foundation for Public Policy Research.*

The awareness of media enslavement is now entrenched within the consciousness of the American people. The treasure trove of truth is seemingly endless: the darkness of government, its bureaucracy, and its secrets. WikiLeaks and other brave individuals have freed people from the enslavement of the so-called free press. WikiLeaks has reinforced the people's right to know. Once the people know, the need to enforce self-governance and hold their United States representative republic accountable is up to the citizenry.

Few would have predicted that WikiLeaks would be freeing Americans from enslavement by the mainstream media. If the Free Press has officially enslaved the American people and beyond; then WikiLeaks and people aligned with it would be the modern day abolitionists running the Underground Railroad.

A free press has responsibility. It must serve the people by being the people's investigator—and do so in a non-partisan way. A free press is critical to a representative Republic, for people must have access to all the knowledge—accurate and unbiased knowledge—

"Moments of Truth: The Free Speech Movement of 2016," by Monica Morrill, Selous Foundation for Public Policy Research, October 19, 2016. Reprinted by permission.

in order to exercise their vote with the judgment they deserve—a judgment based on knowing the facts, not the spin.

What would our Founding Fathers think? What would George Washington and Benjamin Franklin do? On the one hand, young Washington's geographical surveying experience prepared him for potential battlefields to face any army, yet young Franklin's reputation of listening and interacting with people, surveying words and ideas, printing and distributing, guaranteed a rhetorical confrontation with the British. It is upon these foundations of the United States that we must revisit the right to freedom of speech.

Reasserting the right to free speech is nothing new. It is enshrined in the U.S. Constitution, which exists to fulfill the promises of the Declaration of Independence. The First Amendment reads, "Congress shall make no law . . . abridging the freedom of speech, or of the press;" Notice, it reads, "the freedom of speech," necessarily asserting that "the" freedom of speech, the right to using words, pre-existed the Constitution. The freedom of expression and telling the truth begins with the advent of the spoken word.

The media has hijacked this freedom and instead of recognizing the duty of the press to the public, it has renamed it "freedom of the press" as if journalism can tower in lofty imperial offices over the people. The mainstream media correspond with their King and Queen, Obama and Clinton, to ensure that there is no offense to their royal highnesses before publication. That is partially what WikiLeaks has revealed over the past several weeks. The awareness of media enslavement is now infused within the consciousness of the American people. The trust is all but gone between the press and the citizenry they were meant to serve because the media is complicit and entangled in the web of lies, even confabulating stories about Clinton's political opponent Trump. The mainstream media is having a love affair with the Clinton's long-standing political machine and their young King Obama. WikiLeaks has upset the imperious politicians and removed Obama's crown, while denying Clinton hers with the Podesta e-mails, all citizens should at least read the summary to be armed with the facts.

And yet, the citizenry eagerly waits for more truth from WikiLeaks because at least two branches of the Federal government: the Executive Branch and the Judicial Branch have stolen a "free press" that should only answer to the people. Obama has gone wild with Executive Orders to his demise, and by all accounts, thus far, the Judicial Branch is legislating from the bench.

It's not surprising that the mainstream media isn't reporting on WikiLeaks, here are just a couple of topics in the Podesta e-mails: how to undermine Congressman Trey Gowdy in his investigation of Benghazi in a television interview on Face the Nation; and knowledge that "Eric McFadden, who was Hillary's Catholic liaison in the primaries was arrested yesterday for running a prostitution ring. The transition people know" [meaning those hiring people in what would be Queen Clinton's new government already have knowledge of the scandal]. Most recently, it was revealed that someone in the International Operations Division (IOD) of the FBI "pressured" a man to change the classified email to unclassified. The IOD "had been contacted by Patrick Kennedy, Undersecretary of State, who had asked his assistance in altering the email's classification in exchange for a 'quid pro quo'... in exchange for marking the email unclassified, STATE [Department] would reciprocate by allowing the FBI to place more Agents in countries where they are presently forbidden ... KENNEDY spent the next 15 minutes debating the classification of the email and attempting to influence the FBI to change its markings" thus proving that in the United States today the law doesn't matter, but political power and influence does.

More than ever during a polarizing presidential election, an independent press is needed to inform the public. There is a dearth of great journalists today. A free press seems to forget they are not free of responsibility. Genuinely impartial broadcasting is beholden to journalism meant for the people, not reporting in favor of the elite. News sources are expected to be the number one public defender and investigator. Just last Sunday Americans gathered in front of Independence Hall, Philadelphia to declare their desire for the public to know the facts among other things, they were not "with Her" as the mainstream press is.

What we are witnessing this election year is the end of the old world press as we know it; the demise of leaders who only serve themselves while ignoring the needs of the people; complicit government Executive and Judicial Branches who conspire with the Clintons to seize a White House that will never belong to them, because the people are taking it back. The treasure trove of truth is seemingly endless: the darkness of government, its bureaucracy, and its secrets. WikiLeaks and other brave individuals have freed people from the enslavement of the so-called free press. WikiLeaks has reinforced the people's right to know. Once the people know, the need to enforce self-governance and hold their United States representative Republic accountable is up to the citizenry.

7

From Now On, We Can't Pretend We Don't Know

Slavoj Zizek

Slavoj Zizek is a senior researcher at the Institute of Sociology and Philosophy at the University of Ljubljana, global distinguished professor of German at New York University, and international director of the Birkbeck Institute for the Humanities at the University of London.

Perhaps Americans have known for a long time that their government has engaged in activities they should not exactly be proud of. But with the revelations leaked by WikiLeaks, Americans not only have confirmation of those suspicions but also they have been confronted with the dirty details of their leaders' deeds. The creation of WikiLeaks has blown apart the illusion of Western liberty, but has that benefitted society? Is ignorance bliss, or have we entered a new era of political consciousness?

We remember anniversaries that mark the important events of our era: September 11 (not only the 2001 Twin Towers attack, but also the 1973 military coup against Allende in Chile), D-day, etc. Maybe another date should be added to this list: 19 June.

Most of us like to take a stroll during the day to get a breath of fresh air. There must be a good reason for those who cannot do it—maybe they have a job that prevents it (miners, submariners),

"How WikiLeaks Opened Our Eyes to the Illusion of Freedom," by Slavoj Zizek, Alternet, June 19, 2014. ©Guardian News & Media Ltd 2017. Reprinted by permission.

or a strange illness that makes exposure to sunlight a deadly danger. Even prisoners get their daily hour's walk in fresh air.

Today, 19 June, marks two years since Julian Assange was deprived of this right: he is permanently confined to the apartment that houses the Ecuadorian embassy in London. Were he to step out of the apartment, he would be arrested immediately. What did Assange do to deserve this? In a way, one can understand the authorities: Assange and his whistleblowing colleagues are often accused of being traitors, but they are something much worse (in the eyes of the authorities).

Assange designated himself a "spy for the people." "Spying for the people" is not a simple betrayal (which would instead mean acting as a double agent, selling our secrets to the enemy); it is something much more radical. It undermines the very principle of spying, the principle of secrecy, since its goal is to make secrets public. People who help WikiLeaks are no longer whistleblowers who denounce the illegal practices of private companies (banks, and tobacco and oil companies) to the public authorities; they denounce to the wider public these public authorities themselves.

We didn't really learn anything from WikiLeaks we didn't already presume to be true—but it is one thing to know it in general and another to get concrete data. It is a little bit like knowing that one's sexual partner is playing around. One can accept the abstract knowledge of it, but pain arises when one learns the steamy details, when one gets pictures of what they were doing.

When confronted with such facts, should every decent US citizen not feel deeply ashamed? Until now, the attitude of the average citizen was hypocritical disavowal: we preferred to ignore the dirty job done by secret agencies. From now on, we can't pretend we don't know.

It is not enough to see WikiLeaks as an anti-American phenomenon. States such as China and Russia are much more oppressive than the US. Just imagine what would have happened to someone like Chelsea Manning in a Chinese court. In all probability, there would be no public trial; she would just disappear.

The US doesn't treat prisoners as brutally—because of its technological priority, it simply does not need the openly brutal approach (which it is more than ready to apply when needed). But this is why the US is an even more dangerous threat to our freedom than China: its measures of control are not perceived as such, while Chinese brutality is openly displayed.

In a country such as China the limitations of freedom are clear to everyone, with no illusions about it. In the US, however, formal freedoms are guaranteed, so that most individuals experience their lives as free and are not even aware of the extent to which they are controlled by state mechanisms. Whistleblowers do something much more important than stating the obvious by way of denouncing the openly oppressive regimes: they render public the unfreedom that underlies the very situation in which we experience ourselves as free.

Back in May 2002, it was reported that scientists at New York University had attached a computer chip able to transmit elementary signals directly to a rat's brain—enabling scientists to control the rat's movements by means of a steering mechanism, as used in a remote-controlled toy car. For the first time, the free will of a living animal was taken over by an external machine.

How did the unfortunate rat experience its movements, which were effectively decided from outside? Was it totally unaware that its movements were being steered? Maybe therein lies the difference between Chinese citizens and us, free citizens of western, liberal countries: the Chinese human rats are at least aware they are controlled, while we are the stupid rats strolling around unaware of how our movements are monitored.

Is WikiLeaks pursuing an impossible dream? Definitely not, and the proof is that the world has already changed since its revelations.

Not only have we learned a lot about the illegal activities of the US and other great powers. Not only have the WikiLeaks revelations put secret services on the defensive and set in motion legislative acts to better control them. WikiLeaks has achieved much more: millions of ordinary people have become aware of the society in which they live. Something that until now we silently tolerated as unproblematic is rendered problematic.

This is why Assange has been accused of causing so much harm. Yet there is no violence in what WikiLeaks is doing. We all know the classic scene from cartoons: the character reaches a precipice but goes on running, ignoring the fact that there is no ground underfoot; they start to fall only when they look down and notice the abyss. What WikiLeaks is doing is just reminding those in power to look down.

The reaction of all too many people, brainwashed by the media, to WikiLeaks' revelations could best be summed up by the memorable lines of the final song from Altman's film *Nashville*: "You may say I ain't free but it don't worry me." WikiLeaks does make us worry. And, unfortunately, many people don't like that.

8

WikiLeaks Is an Enemy of Open Society

Steven Aftergood

Steven Aftergood directs the FAS Project on Government Secrecy, which works to reduce the scope of national security secrecy and promote public access to government information. He is best known for being the plaintiff in a Freedom of Information Act lawsuit in 1997 against the Central Intelligence Agency that led to the declassification and publication of the total intelligence budget for the first time in fifty years.

WikiLeaks wants to be known as a whistleblowers' site that advocates for open government and the elimination of corruption. But if that is true, then why do other anticorruption groups turn their backs on WikiLeaks? It's true that WikiLeaks has leaked important documents that did not need to be kept classified and that honored the organization's mission of transparency. The problem is that WikiLeaks has no code, and it is as willing to infringe on the rights of individuals even as it exposes government corruption. We can't trust WikiLeaks and its leadership to make the right and ethical choices when it comes to secure information and government security.

In the past week, both the *Washington Post* and the *New York Times* have referred to WikiLeaks.org, the web site that publishes confidential records, as a "whistleblower" site. This conforms to WikiLeaks' own instructions to journalists that "WikiLeaks should

"Wikileaks Fails 'Due Diligence,'" by Steven Aftergood, Federation of American Scientists, June 28, 2010. Reprinted by permission.

be described, depending on context, as the 'open government group', 'anti-corruption group', 'transparency group' or 'whistleblower's site.'"

But calling WikiLeaks a whistleblower site does not accurately reflect the character of the project. It also does not explain why others who are engaged in open government, anti-corruption and whistleblower protection activities are wary of WikiLeaks or disdainful of it. And it does not provide any clue why the Knight Foundation, the preeminent foundation funder of innovative First Amendment and free press initiatives, might have rejected WikiLeaks' request for financial support, as it recently did.

From one perspective, WikiLeaks is a creative response to a real problem afflicting the U.S. and many other countries, namely the over-control of government information to the detriment of public policy. WikiLeaks has published a considerable number of valuable official records that had been kept unnecessarily secret and were otherwise unavailable, including some that I had attempted and failed to obtain myself. Its most spectacular disclosure was the formerly classified videotape showing an attack by a U.S. Army helicopter crew in Baghdad in 2007 which led to the deaths of several non-combatants. Before mostly going dormant late last year, it also published numerous documents that have no particular policy significance or that were already placed in the public domain by others (including a few that were taken from the FAS web site).

WikiLeaks says that it is dedicated to fighting censorship, so a casual observer might assume that it is more or less a conventional liberal enterprise committed to enlightened democratic policies. But on closer inspection that is not quite the case. In fact, WikiLeaks must be counted among the enemies of open society because it does not respect the rule of law nor does it honor the rights of individuals.

Last year, for example, WikiLeaks published the "secret ritual" of a college women's sorority called Alpha Sigma Tau. Now Alpha Sigma Tau (like several other sororities "exposed" by WikiLeaks) is not known to have engaged in any form of misconduct, and

WikiLeaks does not allege that it has. Rather, WikiLeaks chose to publish the group's confidential ritual just because it could. This is not whistleblowing and it is not journalism. It is a kind of information vandalism.

In fact, WikiLeaks routinely tramples on the privacy of non-governmental, non-corporate groups for no valid public policy reason. It has published private rites of Masons, Mormons and other groups that cultivate confidential relations among their members. Most or all of these groups are defenseless against WikiLeaks' intrusions. The only weapon they have is public contempt for WikiLeaks' ruthless violation of their freedom of association, and even that has mostly been swept away in a wave of uncritical and even adulatory reporting about the brave "open government," "whistleblower" site.

On occasion, WikiLeaks has engaged in overtly unethical behavior. Last year, without permission, it published the full text of the highly regarded 2009 book about corruption in Kenya called "It's Our Turn to Eat" by investigative reporter Michela Wrong (as first reported by Chris McGreal in The Guardian on April 9). By posting a pirated version of the book and making it freely available, WikiLeaks almost certainly disrupted sales of the book and made it harder for Ms. Wrong and other anti-corruption reporters to perform their important work and to get it published. Repeated protests and pleas from the author were required before WikiLeaks (to its credit) finally took the book offline.

"Soon enough," observed Raffi Khatchadourian in a long profile of WikiLeaks' Julian Assange in The New Yorker (June 7), "Assange must confront the paradox of his creation: the thing that he seems to detest most–power without accountability–is encoded in the site's DNA, and will only become more pronounced as WikiLeaks evolves into a real institution."

Much could be forgiven to WikiLeaks if it were true that its activities were succeeding in transforming government information policy in favor of increased openness and accountability— as opposed to merely generating reams of publicity for itself.

WikiLeaks supporter Glenn Greenwald of Salon.com wrote that when it comes to combating government secrecy, "nobody is doing that as effectively as WikiLeaks." But he neglected to spell out exactly what effect WikiLeaks has had. Which U.S. government programs have been cancelled as a result of Wikileaks' activities? Which government policies have been revised? How has public discourse shifted? (And, by the way, who has been injured by its work?)

A less sympathetic observer might conclude that WikiLeaks has squandered much of the impact that it might have had.

A telling comparison can be made between WikiLeaks' publication of the Iraq Apache helicopter attack video last April and The New Yorker's publication of the Abu Ghraib abuse photographs in an article by Seymour Hersh in May 2004. Both disclosures involved extremely graphic and disturbing images. Both involved unreleased or classified government records. And both generated a public sensation. But there the similarity ends. The Abu Ghraib photos prompted lawsuits, congressional hearings, courts martial, prison sentences, declassification initiatives, and at least indirectly a revision of U.S. policy on torture and interrogation. By contrast, the WikiLeaks video tendentiously packaged under the title "Collateral Murder" produced none of that—no investigation (other than a leak investigation), no congressional hearings, no lawsuits, no tightening of the rules of engagement. Just a mild scolding from the Secretary of Defense, and an avalanche of publicity for WikiLeaks.

Of course, it's hard for anyone to produce a specific desired outcome from the national security bureaucracy, and maybe WikiLeaks can't be faulted for failing to have done so. But with the whole world's attention at its command for a few days last April, it could have done more to place the focus on the victims of the incident that it had documented, perhaps even establishing a charitable fund to assist their families. But that's not what it chose to do. Instead, the focus remained firmly fixed on WikiLeaks itself and its own ambitious fundraising efforts.

In perhaps the first independent review of the WikiLeaks project, the John S. and James L. Knight Foundation considered and rejected an application from WikiLeaks for financial support. The Knight Foundation was actively looking for grantees who could promote innovative uses of digital technology in support of the future development of journalism. At the end of the process, more than $2.7 million was awarded to 12 promising recipients. WikiLeaks was not among them.

"Every year some applications that are popular among advisors don't make the cut after Knight staff conducts due diligence," said Knight Foundation spokesman Marc Fest in response to an inquiry from Yahoo news. "WikiLeaks was not recommended by Knight staff to the board."

9

WikiLeaks Risks Your Freedoms

Päivikki Karhula

Päivikki Karhula is the chief information specialist in electronic resources at the Library of the Finnish Parliament.

WikiLeaks complicates the nature of privileged and secure information. Opinions are divided about the service provided by such leaks and the repercussions that will result across many sectors. It is essential the public remember data made available by WikiLeaks may also be used as a case to support new bills, surveillance practices, and use of technologies that extend capabilities of censorship and data surveillance. WikiLeaks purports to value an open society, but, ironically, a pervasive fear of being "outed" or revealed by organizations such as WikiLeaks might result in an uncooperative or closed society.

WikiLeaks is an international non-profit organization working for transparency which publishes news leaks based on their ethical, historical and political significance. WikiLeaks was founded in 2006 by Chinese dissidents, journalists and mathematicians, and start-up company technologists from the United States, Taiwan, South Africa Australia, and Europe. An Australian Internet activist, Julian Assange, is described as a director of WikiLeaks.

WikiLeaks was originally launched as a wiki site, but it has moved towards a more traditional publication model and their

"What Is the Effect of WikiLeaks for Freedom of Information?" by Päivikki Karhula, IFLA, October 5, 2012. https://www.ifla.org/publications/what-is-the-effect-of-wikileaks-for-freedom-of-information. Licensed under CC BY 4.0.

texts are edited only by editors. Their database covered more than 1.2 million documents by 2007.

On their website WikiLeaks states *Article 19 of the Universal Declaration of Human Rights* as a basis their work by defining the human rights of expression and receipt of information regardless of frontiers as civil rights. The WikiLeaks web site further defines "principled leaking," as necessary to fight government, individual and corporate corruption. Julian Assange also has compared his actions to Daniel Ellsberg and the Pentagon Papers case as an example of why principled leaking would be necessary for good government.[1]

What Do the Recent WikiLeaks Documents Address?

The most high-profile documents hosted by WikiLeaks are either US based documents or they focus on alleged US government misbehavior. Many of them relate to hidden war crimes or prisoner abuse. The following sections describe the content and value of leaked publications and public reactions on the leaks.

In March 2007 WikiLeaks published the US military's operating manual for the Guantanamo prison camp (Standard Operating Procedures for Camp Delta). The manual indicated that some prisoners were placed outside the areas which members from the International Committee of the Red Cross were allowed to visit. This was something the military has repeatedly denied.

In July 2010, WikiLeaks released *Afghan War Diary*, a compilation of more than 76,900 documents about the War in Afghanistan which were not previously available to the public. These documents indicated that the deaths of innocent civilians at the hands of international forces were covered up.

In October 2010, WikiLeaks released a package of almost 400,000 documents called the *Iraq War Logs* in coordination with major commercial media organizations. US officials confirmed that this was the largest leak of US military secrets in history. The "war logs" showed alleged evidence of torture that was ignored, and that there were more than 109,000 violent deaths between 2004 and 2009 including 66,081 civilians.[2]

On November 28th 2010, WikiLeaks began releasing US State Department diplomatic cables. The New York Times, Le Monde, Der Spiegel, The Guardian and El Pais in co-operation with WikiLeaks published the first articles which revealed that over 250,000 confidential documents had been leaked to WikiLeaks. During the same night the first 219 documents of the diplomatic cables were published on the WikiLeaks website. According to WikiLeaks, all cables will be published during the coming months. By the 4th of December 2010 over 800 cables had been published.[3]

The diplomatic cables originated from Siprnet (Secret Internet Network), a closed network of the US Department of Defense. Over the past ten years US Embassies worldwide were plugged into Siprnet in an effort to increase information sharing. Documents were available on Siprnet for over 2 million people including all military staff. About 100,000 of the leaked cables were labeled "confidential", about 15.000 had the higher classification "secret", but there were no documents classified as "top secret" on the classification scale.[4]

Reactions to Diplomatic Cable Leaks

Leaking the content of US diplomatic cables caused dramatically harder reactions in different countries than any other of the earlier actions of WikiLeaks. It made also civil rights organizations reconsider their stand on WikiLeaks.

On December 6th US Attorney General Eric Holder announced that WikiLeaks was under criminal investigation and that there could be prosecutions of individuals for leaking classified documents. Julian Assange, director of WikiLeaks, was arrested 7th December 2010 in Britain and accused of sexual assaults in Sweden. However, he was released 16th December against bail for a home arrest. No charges due to the leaks have been filed so far against him.

WikiLeaks also became as a target of attacks and blocks. Immediately after the documents were published, a denial-of-service (DoS) attack was carried out against the WikiLeaks website. WikiLeaks was blocked by government organizations and service providers in China, UAE, Australia (on a black list), Switzerland (by a US service provider) and in the USA (from Federal Government staff, Library of Congress, Department of Education). Also, in California WikiLeaks was temporarily blocked from all DNS addresses after the cable leaks.

Several financial institutions, including Swiss PostFinance, PayPal, Bank of America, Visa and MasterCard, closed WikiLeaks' accounts shortly after the cables were published. These events were followed by DoS attacks against MasterCard and Visa which were organized by activists defending WikiLeaks. As a consequence of this attack Facebook and Twitter also closed the accounts and pages used by hackers.[5] As such, these reactions increased concerns about the tactics of WikiLeaks.

Direct censorship by blocking was not the only restrictive reaction against WikiLeaks. In USA university students as well as government staff and prospective employees were warned by the State Department not to read, print, comment on or make links to WikiLeaks.[6] The reasoning behind this warning was that the data in WikiLeaks is still officially held as classified.[7]

Government Reactions to WikiLeaks

US government reactions to WikiLeaks have hardened over time. Concerning Afghan War Diary, the Pentagon pressured WikiLeaks to return all documents. The Iraq War Logs leak in 2010 was condemned by the US and UK who suggested the disclosures put lives at risk.

The leak of the diplomatic cables in November 2010 naturally caused more reactions in different countries than any other items WikiLeaks had published, since it also touched sensitive political issues for different governments.

US policymakers have been both critical and supportive of WikiLeaks' actions. Secretary of State Hillary Clinton decried immediately the illegal publication of classified documents from government computers, and defended the need for "confidential space" for diplomatic conversations. In addition, she noted that people's lives could be endangered by confidential data disclosures.[8]

However, other governments' reactions were considerably milder concerning the possible impacts of the leaks. According to US Defense Secretary Robert Gates the leaks were embarrassing but he estimated that they would only have "modest" consequences for US foreign policy.[9]

German Interior Minister Thomas de Maizière described WikiLeaks as irritating and annoying for Germany, but not a threat. However, he also defended governments' position to hold secret information, saying "Governments also have to be able to communicate confidentially. Confidentiality and transparency are not mutually exclusive, but rather two sides of the same coin."[10]

In Finland politicians' reactions were controversial. Minister of Foreign Affairs, Alexande Stubb, described the leaks as regrettable and stated "I support transparency and public diplomacy. However, some information between states can be sensitive. This is certainly a difficult situation."[11]

Former Minister of Foreign Affairs, Erkki Tuomioja, emphasized that leaking of diplomatic cables was based on stealing of data and he saw WikiLeaks activities in this case as questionable. On the other hand, one member of the parliament, Annika Lapintie (Left Alliance) proposed a Nobel Prize for WikiLeaks.[12]

Divided Opinions Among Civil Rights Organizations

WikiLeaks has also become a dividing and controversial issue also among civil rights organizations. Many organizations agree on the undeniable value that WikiLeaks has had by indicating violations of human rights and civil liberties. According to Glenn Greenwald, lawyer and civil rights activist, the amount of corruption which WikiLeaks has exposed is unique in history and there is no other organization that comes close to WikiLeaks regarding exposures of misuse of power.[13]

Many civil right organizations have so far openly supported the work of WikiLeaks because of these reasons. The reasoning behind their support is based on the fair rules and justified functionality of democracy and civil society. If secrecy of administrative documents is used to cover government misbehavior, especially inhuman conditions and killing of people, there must be legal grounds to overcome formal borders of secrecy. This has seen as a justified way to protect democratic society and citizen against secret arbitrary government power.

However, the leaks of diplomatic cables made some civil rights organizations and activists back off with their full support for WikiLeaks. The Afghan War Diary leaks had already been harshly criticised by Reporters without Borders. They accused WikiLeaks of "incredible irresponsibility." Although they admitted that WikiLeaks "has in the past played a useful role" by exposing violations of human rights and civil liberties, the case of Afghan War Diary was to some extent different. WikiLeaks was accused of revealing the identity of hundreds of people who collaborated with the coalition in Afghanistan and making them vulnerable for further violence.[14]

Although there is largely an agreement about the value of leaked information, the strategies, tactics and mistakes of WikiLeaks have gained critics. It has also been questioned if the impact of the leaks will lead in an opposite direction than was expected: towards more secrecy and increasing restrictions. Stephen Aftergood, director of Federation of American Scientists Project on Government Secrecy comments: "It has invaded personal privacy. It has published libellous material. It has violated intellectual property rights. And above all, it has launched a sweeping attack not simply on corruption, but on secrecy itself. And I think that's both a strategic and a tactical error. It's a strategic error because some secrecy is perfectly legitimate and desirable. It's a tactical error because it has unleashed a furious response from the US government and other governments that I fear is likely to harm the interests of a lot of other people besides WikiLeaks who are concerned with open government. It may become harder to support protection for people who disclose and publish classified information after WikiLeaks."[15]

Altogether, debate on WikiLeaks has become very complex. There seems to be a pressure on taking sides for or against WikiLeaks or giving statements for them. However, it will require an analytic discussion to recognize both pros and cons in their activities.

It is somewhat difficult for civil society organizations to make clear statements for several reasons. Firstly, WikiLeaks' political activities have taken different shapes during last years and even many transparency activists are not behind all of them. While it is unquestionable that leaks about war crimes and prison violence have given valuable information for society, it is harder to judge the value of data from large amount of diplomatic cables.

It would require weighing an undeniable efficiency of WikiLeaks' actions and validity of concerns they have revealed against their provocative and questionable ways of political action. "There is an alternative mechanism for progress," suggested Stephen Aftergood, "So it's really not a question of WikiLeaks or nothing. It's a question of a smart, well-targeted approach or a reckless shotgun approach."[16]

Impact of the Cable Leaks on Intellectual Freedom

What is the possible impact of WikiLeaks? Is it going to increase or restore the space of free speech or advance transparency of public documents? Or is it going to have the opposite effect and make governments strengthen their restrictions and increase different forms of Internet censorship?

There are several valid concerns and evident signs about stricter legislation and more in depth surveillance practices which may find their grounds on WikiLeaks. Shortly after cable leaks three

US senators (Ensign, Lieberman, Brown) introduced a bill aimed at stopping WikiLeaks by making it illegal to publish the names of military or intelligence community informants. According to Brown, The Securing Human Intelligence and Enforcing Lawful Dissemination Act (SHIELD) would prevent anyone from compromising national security in the future in a similar manner to WikiLeaks.[17]

Another bill under discussion would give the US government extended rights to wiretap all online communication and Internet traffic including foreign-based service providers. The wiretapping bill would also require software developers which enable peer-to-peer communication to redesign their service to allow interception.[18] Concerns have been raised if WikiLeaks is used to gain support for this legislation.[19]

In early December 2010 US senators Joe Lieberman and Dianne Feinstein invoked the 1917 Espionage Act and urged its use in prosecuting Julian Assange. Liebermann also extended his invocation to include the use of this Act to investigate the New York Times, which published WikiLeaks' diplomatic cables. Naomi Wolf, journalist and civil rights activists, warned about the consequences of this practice: "Assange, let us remember, is the New York Times in the parallel case of the Pentagon Papers, not Daniel Ellsberg; he is the publisher, not the one who revealed the classified information—then any outlet, any citizen, who discusses or addresses 'classified' information can be arrested on 'national security' grounds," concluded Wolf.[20]

Another a crucial issue is the protection of sources. What will happen to journalists' rights to publish leaked information? US lawyer and civil rights activist. Glenn Greenwald condenses this concern soundly: "Put simply, there is no intellectually coherent way to distinguish what WikiLeaks has done with these diplomatic cables with what newspapers around the world did in this case and what they do constantly: namely, receive and then publish classified information without authorization."[21]

The consequences of losing a right to protect sources may lead to extreme transparency, but does it lead to the kind of transparency which would support democracy and civil society? American journalist Claire Berlinski reveals the faulty logic of this kind of philosophy in her statement: "The hypocrisy and double-standard of journalists, in particular, who fail to understand why the government must sometimes protect its sources of information is mind-blowing. Journalists, of all people, should understand this better than anyone else. Many sources would lose their jobs, their reputations, their liberty or their lives for talking to journalists on the record. If the people who spoke to us didn't think we could keep their names out of the story, they would never open their mouths again. Would that make the world more transparent?"[22]

Library and Information Field and WikiLeaks

According to the ALA (American Library Association), WikiLeaks relates to many policy issues including access to government information, censorship and the blocking of web sites, government secrecy and the over-classification of government information, treatment of whistleblowers, government transparency and the legalities surrounding classified information. Presently, it looks like WikiLeaks has raised dozens of political and legal questions which will take time to respond to.[23]

Also, in the library field there have been controversial approaches to WikiLeaks. Library of Congress have blocked access to WikiLeaks, which has raised a vivid debate on censorship among libraries.[24] Consequently, ALA has compiled a proposal for a resolution to support accessibility to WikiLeaks and library associations in other countries are considering the same.[25]

From FAIFE's point of view it would be valuable to focus on the direct and indirect censorship effects of WikiLeaks in different countries, organizations and libraries. However, as indicated, WikiLeaks may also be used as a case to support such new bills, surveillance practices and use of technologies which extend capabilities of censorship and data surveillance. Unfortunately, there is not yet much evidence of the development trend towards another direction: to strengthen transparency and increase the space for freedom of speech within the aftermath of WikiLeaks.

Notes

1 Wikipedia (English). Wikileaks

2 BBC. Wikileaks: Iraq war logs 'reveal truth about conflict. BBC News (bbc.co.uk), 23.10.2010

3 United States Diplomatic Cable Leaks. Wikipedia

4 United States Diplomatic Cable Leaks. Wikipedia

5 The Economist, The War on Wikileaks. Economist.com, 9.12.2010

6 Wikipedia (English). Wikileaks

7 Fishman, Rob, State Department To Columbia University Students: DO NOT Discuss WikiLeaks On Facebook. Twitter, The Huffington Post (huffingtonpost.com), 6.12.2010.

8 Jones, Barbara, Wikileaks and its relationship to ALA.

9 Whitlock, Craig, Gates: Warnings of WikiLeaks fallout overblown. The Washington Post (voices.washingtonpost.com), 30.11.2010.

10 Stark, Holger & Rosenbach, Marcel, WikiLeaks Is Annoying, But Not a Threat. Spiegel Online, 20.12.2010

11 YLE. Finland Surfaces in Wikileaks Exposé. YLE.fi, 29.11.2010

12 Wikipedia (Finnish). Wikileaks

13 Is WikiLeaks' Julian Assange a Hero? Glenn Greenwald Debates Steven Aftergood of Secrecy News / Democracy Now (Video & transcript), 3.12.2010

14 Siddique, Haroon, Press freedom group joins condemnation of WikiLeaks' war logs. The Guardian (guardian.co.uk), 13.8.2010.

15 Is WikiLeaks' Julian Assange a Hero? Glenn Greenwald Debates Steven Aftergood of Secrecy News / Democracy Now (Video & transcript), 3.12.2010

16 Is WikiLeaks' Julian Assange a Hero? Glenn Greenwald Debates Steven Aftergood of Secrecy News / Democracy Now (Video & transcript), 3.12.2010

17 Nagesh, Gautham, Senators unveil anti-WikiLeaks bill. The Hill (thehill.com), 3.12.2010

18 Savage, Charlie, U.S. tries to make it easier to wiretap the Internet. The New York Times (nytimes.com), 27.9.2010.

19 Is The US Response To Wikileaks Really About Overhyping Online Threats To Pass New Laws?, Techdirt, 13.12.2010.

20 Wolf, Naomi, Espionage Act: How the Government Can Engage in Serious Aggression Against the People of the United States, The Huffington Post (huffingtonpost.com), 10.12.2010.

21 Greenwald, Glenn, Attempts to prosecute WikiLeaks endanger press freedoms. Salon (salon.com), 14.12.2010.

22 Pilon, Roger, Keeping WikiLeaks in perspective. Cato @ Liberty (cato-at-liberty.org), 6.12.2010

23 Jones, Barbara, Wikileaks and its relationship to ALA

24 Why the Library of Congress Is Blocking Wikileaks

25 Revised version: Resolution in Support of WikiLeaks (12/29/10)

10

Leaks in the Age of Accountability

James W. Davis and Miriam Meckel

James W. Davis is a professor of international politics at the Institute of Political Science and dean of the School of Economics and Political Science at the University of St. Gallen in Switzerland.

Miriam Meckel is professor for corporate communication and director of the Institute for Media and Communication Management at the University of St. Gallen in Switzerland.

The more documents WikiLeaks has leaked, the more the American public has wondered what the organization's true mission is. Where once a larger percentage of Americans believed the leaks were done in the public interest to make governments more accountable, that number has dwindled with the release of documents that put diplomats and private citizens at risk. WikiLeaks has lost control of the public's perception of its purpose and is unable to effect significant change at the higher levels of government. WikiLeaks, it seems, has a public relations problem.

Discourse

Without a doubt, WikiLeaks has provoked a wide-ranging and sustained debate, but the focus has been less on how to redress power asymmetries between publics and governments in favor of increased political accountability and more on the propriety of state secrets.

"Political Power and the Requirements of Accountability in the Age of WikiLeaks," by Miriam Meckel and James W. Davis, Researchgate.Net, June 2013. Reprinted by permission.

The course of the public debate is in part a function of the way in which WikiLeaks chose to publicize the data that had been leaked to it. In the summer of 2010, over forty percent of Americans thought that the leaks served the public interest. But over time the massive and indiscriminate nature of the leaks led to widespread suspicion among the public that Wikileaks' principal motive was not a desire to uncover specific abuses of public authority. Consequently, by December 2010, only twenty-nine percent of Americans believed that WikiLeaks' releases served the public interest. Almost eighty percent expressed disapproval of the publication of diplomatic and military documents. In a poll conducted for CBS News three fourths of respondents agreed with the statement that "there are some things the public does not have a right to know if it might affect national security" (quoted in Roberts 2012: 19).

These changes in the public's opinion of WikiLeaks presumably result from some failures and misunderstandings regarding the basic mechanisms of information processing and public debate that have evolved with the technological and social innovations related to digitalization and networked communication. WikiLeaks seems to have assumed that leaking is sufficient for producing an informed public and has underestimated the need to seek allies in the process of turning information into knowledge and collective action.

While the organization's name suggests a close relation to other Wiki organizations (e.g. Wikimedia, Wikipedia), there is no such connection. Instead, the Wikimedia Foundation has emphasized the fact that there is no relation between their organization and WikiLeaks, and it's CEO, Jimmy Wales, repeatedly criticized the fact that WikiLeaks might put lives at risk by leaking secret information that reveals the names of involved persons.[1]

Even a cursory analysis shows that the formal prerequisites for a wiki-like collaboration are lacking. For example, there is no evidence that WikiLeaks is a similar collaboration platform to Wikipedia. A wiki is a website that allows anyone to create and edit pages. This is not true for WikiLeaks. The documents on the website are mostly written by Julian Assange (if there have been other authors there is no transparent information about it). There is no opportunity for random people to edit or comment on WikiLeaks documents. Thus, WikiLeaks is not a wiki (Beutler 2010). The organization has not taken advantage of one of the basic technology-based innovations in collaboration via communication provided by the internet: the involvement of users as contributors in pursuit of crowdsourcing and broadening the platform's legitimation.

WikiLeaks has also failed to establish durable alliances with NGOs or the media in order to build a solid network of actors and protagonists committed to using technology to support the free flow of information and public awareness of relevant facts in national and international politics. Rather, beginning in 2010, the platform increasingly limited its activities to targeting the US government, not only by leaking problematic and embarrassing information, but also by stereotyping it as an enemy of freedom of information. In doing so, WikiLeaks itself contributed to a shift in public perception. It is no longer universally seen to be a "good" organization taking action against "bad," i.e. non democratic governments, but increasingly regarded as an ambiguous actor in an undefined battle for political, economic or military secrets.

Finally, Julian Assange has destroyed the close connection between WikiLeaks and the media that helped to promote a series of "scoops"—from the release of the "Collateral Murder" video to the "Afghan War Diaries" and "Iraq War Logs" (all in 2010). Assange seems at some point to have turned into a digital road warrior, restricting the activities of WikiLeaks to a digital road ahead; one that is not, however, open to all citizens. But as research on the "source cycle" between digital agenda setting via weblogs, twitter and Facebook and the agenda of traditional media has shown (Messner/DiStaso 2008), it does not make much sense to refrain from including the respective other in one's own agenda setting activities. By ignoring the fact that a data platform needs the traditional media to spread information widely to less well connected groups of citizens and by even starting to fight some of the media that had before been "partners in crime" Julian Assange forfeited the chance to establish WikiLeaks as a durable component of the "source cycle."

WikiLeaks has focused on leaking data, an approach that—at least from a formal standpoint—reveals some parallels to open data strategies in networked politics, such as those promoted by the Obama administration since 2009. Both approaches provide data in an attempt to empower the recipients, who can use it for their own good. But there is a major difference: open data from governmental organizations is provided in the context of institutionalized agreements over political processes and the rule of law (see above). This is not true for WikiLeaks.

The organization has not even tried to establish sustainable links between the act of leaking and the further processing of information. It has also failed to recognize how crowd sourcing might become an element of transformational communication strategies that support political accountability. It has neglected its original affiliations with mass media and has managed to spoil several relations with experts in education, academia and even the political system, as doubts about the integrity of the organization and its founder, Julian Assange, have arisen and caused former supporters to turn into critics.

In terms of *discourse*, WikiLeaks could have played a different role in establishing a relationship to other parts and actors in the overall agenda setting process in society. Over the long run, it could have produced a major change in a digitally networked media ecosystem. Instead, WikiLeaks, in particular Julian Assange, has tried to monopolized authority over interpreting the leaked data, to control information about the data and the organization WikiLeaks itself, and has neglected to apply the mechanisms of the new media ecosystem, which are based on collaboration and "coopetition", to the very work of his organization.

Transparency and Accountability: Some Lessons Learned and Some Requirements

WikiLeaks gave rise to great and far reaching hopes and expectations for changing the somewhat numbed conversation between the representatives of political power and citizens in an increasingly abstract public sphere. And, indeed, some of the first leaks appeared to empower the public to challenge perceived failures in political, economic and societal accountability. WikiLeaks seemed to incarnate the promises of the networked digital age and its transformational influence on power, policy and accountability: "WikiLeaks is just one piece of a much larger continuum of changes in how the people and the powerful relate to each other in this new time—changes that are fundamentally healthy for the growth and strength of an open society. Secrecy and the hoarding of information are ending; openness and the sharing of information are coming" (Sifry 2011: 17).

There might be such a continuum. But more will be needed than a call for total transparency and a religious-like belief in unconventional organizations (Karafyllis 2010). Challenging "the formal functioning of power," as Žižek (2011) puts it, alone cannot transform *and advance* the relationship between policy makers and their stakeholders. Instead, building a solid platform for dialogue and interaction that is open to different groups of actors which are involved in the agenda setting process of the public sphere and endorsing it through clear and transparent processes would appear to offer a much more promising way forward.

Returning to our three-step-model of collective political empowerment (OECD 2001) and combining it with the above mentioned communications science model that sees an evolution of data to information and information to knowledge, we can generate a matrix that helps to identify and distinguish among a variety of social practices relevant to a discussion of how WikiLeaks might contribute to more accountability.

The forgoing analysis suggests that five of the nine social practices identified here facilitate wide-scale public education and participation in political communication: 1) the traditional information supply by the *mass media*; 2) *open data* initiatives that provide a means for citizens to consult with one another; 3) integrating citizens into data gathering via *crowd sourcing*; 4) turning this into an institutionalized approach of *open government*; 5) establishing a system of *liquid democracy* in which the basic negotiation processes are all based on permanent interactions between people, organizations and governments (Vogelmann 2012; Hernani 2011).

To date, WikiLeaks has been involved in only one of the strategically relevant practices. By cooperating with media institutions WikiLeaks has managed to at least enter the second field (mass media). Moreover, while one might argue that the organization has boosted public discourse on open data and led to increased lobbying in favor of fewer restrictions on government information, neither of these effects has led to increased political accountability. Why is that so? Because leaking itself neither provides for the contextual information necessary for an informed public nor facilitates new forms of political participation. With regard to the above depicted geography of the digitalized public sphere, WikiLeaks has not reached beyond the information column—a modest result for an organization that once regarded itself as the harbinger of revolutionary political communication and change.

It would seem that political power—as well as the possibility for challenging it—requires an institutionalized rational foundation that is not exposed to constant or sudden change. The case of the former German defense minister, Karl-Theodor zu Guttenberg, is illustrative. The original charge that zu Guttenberg's doctoral dissertation was plagued by wide-scale plagiarism arose in the context of an academic book review. Thereafter, mainstream media drew attention to the charge. Evidence documenting the plagiarism was collected and disseminated via the internet platform GuttenPlag. Ultimately, however, zu Guttenberg was held accountable for his breach of academic (and legal) standards by means of a regulated proceeding (*geregeltes Verfahren*) within the University of Bayreuth (Preuß/Schultz 2011: 107).

By contrast, because it leads to uncertainty and a lack of reliability, the ideology of total transparency will not improve and expand dialogue in support of political accountability. Rather, it is likely to lead people to refrain from participating in the public sphere altogether, setting off another feedback loop such as the one caused by the "Cablegate" leaks.

Finally, an organization that is accountable only to itself is hardly in the position to effect changes in the level of political accountability in democratic societies. These require extending the standards and rules to all relevant levels of decision making. A moral authority of a population n=1 cannot have a legitimate impact on society. WikiLeaks might be "an extraordinarily clever hack of the world's legal system" (Economist 2010), but one that will suffer from shortcomings in the standards of the very parameter it claimed to support: political accountability.

Notes

1. "I wish they wouldn't use the name, they are not a Wiki", he said at a business conference in Kuala Lumpur, according to AFP (http://articles.nydailynews.com/2010-09-28/news/27076688_1_wikile aks-jimmy-wales-military-documents; Accessed 10.5.2013).

11

WikiLeaks Endangers Our Intelligence Community

Joshua Foust

Joshua Foust is a journalist, speaker, and former intelligence analyst. Currently, he is a national security fellow at the Foreign Policy Research Institute.

It is one thing to leak information that holds a powerful nation's government accountable, but should individuals be fair game for similar treatment? Some leaked documents have named confidential sources of diplomats. Not only can this put individuals at risk, it can have potentially even farther-reaching effects, such as compromising the operations of the intelligence community. WikiLeaks has a responsibility to censor information that puts innocent people at risk and, most important, should be held accountable when it fails to do so.

The Wikileaked embassy cables have been viewed as either the foreign policy equivalent of TMZ or as the ruination of the entire international system. Both stances are wrongheaded. There was never any danger of these cables fundamentally changing the international system, however grandiose the dreams of Julian Assange. Secretary of Defense Bob Gates recently said that every other government on the planet knows the U.S. government "leaks like a sieve." And much like the previous two tranches of secret

"WikiLeaks Hurts the Cause of Transparency," by Joshua Foust, WNET.ORG, December 3, 2010. Reprinted by permission.

documents, these cables do not fundamentally alter anyone's perceptions or understandings of U.S. foreign policy. If anything, they make specific U.S. diplomats, like Anne Patterson, the former ambassador to Pakistan, appear as heroic sages and elder statesmen.

The real issue to consider with the "Cablegate" leaks is what comes next. (Full disclosure: I work for a defense contractor, but these views are mine alone). With the possible exception of Saudi Arabia's bloodlust toward Iran, the big stories in Cablegate are interesting but not terribly compelling. Informed readers and analysts had already theorized almost everything they highlight, so while there is now official confirmation of many pieces of conventional wisdom, the big picture hasn't changed noticeably. So what is the big deal?

The Details Still Matter

I made this same argument when Wikileaks first released its Afghanistan archive in July. Though they don't change the big picture, these documents can be terribly dangerous in individual circumstances. The New York Times reported that many of the cables "name diplomats' confidential sources, from foreign legislators and military officers to human rights activists and journalists," with warnings to please protect their identities. These informants face retribution—potentially violent retribution—if they are exposed. It is why documents are marked secret in the first place: to protect the identity of sources.

And embassy cables contain more than that. When I was deployed to Afghanistan with the U.S. Army Human Terrain System, the U.S. embassy in Kabul would put out warnings in its cables about changes to its security procedures in case we ever needed to visit. If details like those are in these cables, then every embassy that has recently described its security procedures is potentially at risk. A number of American embassies and consulates have been targeted for violence in recent years in surprising places like Serbia, Turkey and Greece, in addition to the usual suspects like Saudi Arabia, Yemen, Pakistan and Afghanistan. It is unconscionable to expose such information, but once again we're left with solemn assurances from information thieves and the good judgment of journalists not to expose it.

There is a common assertion about all three document releases that in the immediate aftermath no one got killed, so there shouldn't be so much concern about the newest round of leaks. But this is silly—one cannot prove a negative. The Taliban recently repeated that they will take action against any informers they can identify from the leaked documents. To say there is no risk from such disclosure is deeply irresponsible, like refusing to wear your seat belt because you have never been in an accident. It is simply too risky.

The Intelligence Community Will Falter

Over the summer, I predicted that one of the major consequences of Wikileaks would be the damage to how the intelligence community (IC) operates. Despite numerous studies recommending change, the IC as a whole is still routinely criticized for not "connecting the dots" sufficiently quickly or rigorously to stop every single attempt to execute a terrorist attack. To connect the dots, you need to be able to see the dots. But in the wake of Wikileaks' reckless exposures of U.S. secrets, agencies are responding by clamping down on access—the precise opposite of enabling the connecting of dots.

On Monday, the State Department announced it was withdrawing its Net Centric Diplomacy database from the SIPRNET, the secret network the cables were originally stolen from. Analysts deployed to other countries, as I was in Afghanistan, rely on embassy cables to report on civilian, political and economic issues (topics that do not normally make it into military reporting channels, which are concerned with issues like tactics and operations). Analysts deployed to other countries very often only have SIPRNET access. While understandable, State's Wikileaks-induced withdrawal from the secret network will adversely affect the intelligence community's ability to collect and understand information. It is a reversal of all the progress toward openness and discoverability the intelligence community had made since 2001.

Similarly, this is going to affect the nature of the cables themselves. A tremendous value in diplomatic reporting is its frankness—an unvarnished, unromantic view of a foreign leader, a process or a specific area. The built-in cynicism of many diplomats is actually quite refreshing to read, especially when compared to how they discuss the same issues and people publicly. That is now under threat. It is a good bet that at least a few relationships—say, with a key ally like Turkey—will become badly stressed because of the disclosure of these cables. In the process, some ambassadors will likely be recalled—what they've said about their counterparts is just too embarrassing for them to remain in their posts.

Being forced to fire an ambassador for doing her job is bad enough. But everyone should worry that future ambassadors and diplomats will tightly censor the content of their assessments back to Washington. That is not only a net loss for the United States —something many cheering the cables' release seem to celebrate —but it makes horrible breakdowns in communication between agencies, like the run up to the Iraq War, more likely.

This Hurts the Cause of Transparency

The natural reaction to theft is paranoia about security. If a thief breaks into your home because you left a window unlocked, it is natural to become paranoid about locking every single entrance to your home as a result. In a very real way, Wikileaks has participated in the theft of classified data. As a result, we can expect the U.S. government to respond by increasing the security around its data, regardless of classification.

The State Department's withdrawal of NCD from SIPRNET is only one example of how this will function. It is not unreasonable to think that new pieces of analysis or intelligence will be classified at ever-higher levels—over the top-secret networks that are much harder to leak into the public. But classifying information more aggressively so fewer people can read it is the opposite of transparency! Even information that is perfectly unclassified will probably be transmitted over the higher-security networks now —the danger of exposing them to leaking is simply too great.

Most of the diplomatic cables in this latest tranche were scheduled to be declassified automatically by 2035 (built into the secret classification system is a time limit). History was not at risk of these cables remaining classified, but if the government responds by classifying information at higher levels, then it could be for everything moving forward.

There's no doubt that these cables are fascinating to read for a variety of reasons. But the risks and challenges they pose—not to the international system or the nature of diplomacy but to whether America can function as its citizens demand—are so great it's difficult to argue that, on balance, these will be a net good. This year has seen Wikileaks do incalculable harm to America. It may soldier on, as Secretary Gates says (we are nothing if not resilient), but the government's ability to function is going to be damaged because of them.

12

Worldwide, Super Injunctions Put Country Before Justice

Binoy Kampmark

Binoy Kampmark is a senior lecturer in the School of Global, Urban, and Social Studies, teaching within the bachelor of social science program at RMIT University in Australia.

Legal suppression and censorship have been the preferred forms of restraint by global governments in dealing with WikiLeaks. In Australia, governments are resorting to using super injunctions to suppress releases to the public. Thanks to the suppression order, journalists are allowed to report on a leaked document, but they may not disclose the contents of the document or discuss why the document was leaked or what damage it may do. Of course, such suppression plays into the very reasons WikiLeaks seeks to blow the whistle on government secrecy.

The Westminster system has always been seen, in some select circles, as a model for freedom and expression. It has been everything but. In Australia, whose institutions do still pride themselves on an antiquated obsession with aspects of English gagging, suppression orders do retain a certain mystique. They certainly do in the Australian state of Victoria, which is said to throw "suppression orders around like confetti."[1]

"Suppression Order and Freedom of Expression: WikiLeaks, Corruption and the Super Injunction," by Dr. Binoy Kampmark, Global Research, August 3, 2014. Reprinted by permission.

The absurdity of its application has become all too evident with the publication by WikiLeaks of the super injunction covering allegations of corruption dealing with leaders from Malaysia, Indonesia and Vietnam. All had multi-million dollar dealings of a purportedly inappropriate nature with subsidiaries of the Reserve Bank of Australia (RBA). These supposedly involved the alleged bribery of foreign officials concerned with banknote printing contracts. The top brass from these countries, including, for instance, "any current or former Prime Minister of Malaysia," "Truong Tan San, currently President of Vietnam," "Susilo Bambang Yudhoyono, currently President of Indonesia (since 2004)," and "Megawati Sukarnoputri, a former President of Indonesia."

The suppression order has formidable currency in the English law canon. It is used to shut people up. It is used to keep silence golden. It is intended as a self-censoring measure that uses the cudgel of the law to keep people, and the media, in tow. WikiLeaks has fronted this legal remedy before, notably in the case of Trafigura[3], a multinational which had been more than happy to use African bases as dumping grounds for its toxic waste. The company attempted, unsuccessfully, to keep discussion of its exploits under wraps.

In the post-analogue age, it remains to be seen how far such orders can genuinely go—there is more than enough oxygen for publicity to go around, and social media has proven positively inflammatory on the subject of the money printing order. Any prosecution against either a social media user or publisher for discussing the case would not only be futile but dangerous. Because of the threat, Australia journalists have been tiptoeing like ballerinas on the subject of what to reveal.

This has meant that journalists in Australia can report that WikiLeaks has released a document disclosing details on a suppression order, but are unable to discuss it without legal consequences. Such details cannot be disclosed, despite the absurd situation of a global conversation taking place on that very order. (Witness, for instance, a vigorous discussion taking place on the order in the Malaysian press.[4]) As with all matters regarding censorship, absurdity, and a good degree of spinelessness, tend to be the only victors.

The super injunction has had several famed appearances. The absurdity was well exposed when it came to such programs as the British quiz show Have I Got News For You. There, the super injunction has been discussed, only to disappear at the behest of legal advice to participants on the program. Ian Hislop, veteran editor of the hilariously wicked Private Eye tended to, as he still does, sail close to the legal wind on several occasions.

The super injunction has certainly been the favoured form of restraint on the press from celebrities. The situation with such figures is far less relevant than that of political subjects—what Ryan Giggs, former Manchester United player did or did not so in his sex life can hardly be said to be a matter of grand public interest. Such figures, in their dubiousness, are certainly entitled to what shreds of privacy they might have left, even if the resort to the Human Rights Act 1998 may seem gratuitous. The same can't be said for political representatives who use their offices to pursue goals outside the remit of their election. Their relationship with constituents is both bond and undertaking.

There are always concessions to be made when allegations are reported. Material alleged has to be material proved. The respective evidentiary onus on the parties has to be discharged. This will happen, it is hoped, in the fullness of time, in so far as time is generous in such proceedings.

But the assumption that the province of law is somehow meditative and hermetic, that it exists outside the time and workings of politics, is at best a childish notion. Embarrassment masquerades as matters of national security. As the document itself states, "The purpose of these orders is to prevent damage to Australia's international relations that may be caused by the publication of material that may damage the reputations of specified individuals who are not the subject of charges in these proceedings." Naturally, terms such as "justice" are used liberally, though the primary object is less justice than the necessity to "prevent prejudice to the interests of the Commonwealth in relation to national security."

The governments in question—those of Australia, Malaysia, Indonesia and Vietnam—want silence on the matter. Canberra is particularly worried, feeling that their business partners might be unnecessarily impugned. They have managed, in part, to secure that reticence through the channel of Australian, and more specifically Victorian, law. They are desperate to chill, if not kill, the matter. Alleged misconduct has effectively been cloaked from public scrutiny.

Time and time again, orders of restraint and injunctions have been sought to restrain the publication of information that would have informed public discussion on matters of crucial political performance. That discussion can still, as it should, take place irrespective of whether the charges are proven in court. The very fact that the governments in question are all receiving the comforts of immunity in an Australian court room needs to be seriously questioned. Don't expect Australian media outlets to heed that point.

Notes

1. http://www.crikey.com.au/2014/07/30/wikileaks-reveals-not-so-superinjunction/

2. https://wikileaks.org/aus-suppression-order/

3. http://www.theguardian.com/media/2009/oct/13/trafigura-drops-gag-guardian-oil

4. http://www.themalaymailonline.com/malaysia/article/australia-muzzles-press-on-bribery-case-involving-malaysian-regional-leader

Organizations to Contact

The editors have compiled the following list of organizations concerned with the issues debated in this book. The descriptions are derived from materials provided by the organizations. All have publications or information available for interested readers. The list was compiled on the date of publication of the present volume; the information provided here may change. Be aware that many organizations take several weeks or longer to respond to inquiries, so allow as much time as possible.

Alaveteli
website: http://alaveteli.org

Alaveteli is a resource that allows citizens to request information, and the replies are recorded for all to see on the website. Historic requests, along with any resulting correspondence, are archived publicly online. This increases the availability of the requested information, and encourages transparency. Therefore, Alaveteli acts both as a useful tool for citizens and as an advocacy tool for right-to-know campaigners. Funded by the Open Society Institute and the Hivos Foundation, the project supports FOI websites around the world.

Electronic Frontier Foundation (EFF)
815 Eddy Street
San Francisco, CA 94109 USA
phone: (415) 436-9333
email: info@eff.org
website: www.eff.org

The Electronic Frontier Foundation is the leading nonprofit organization defending civil liberties in the digital world. Founded in 1990, EFF champions user privacy, free expression, and innovation through impact litigation, policy analysis, grassroots activism, and technology development. The EFF works to ensure that rights and freedoms are enhanced and protected as the use of technology grows.

Global Witness
Lloyds Chambers
1 Portsoken Street
London, E1 8BT
United Kingdom
phone: +44 (0)207 4925820
email: mail@globalwitness.org
website: www.globalwitness.org

Many of the world's worst environmental and human rights abuses are driven by the exploitation of natural resources and corruption in the global political and economic system. Global Witness is campaigning to end this. They carry out hard-hitting investigations, expose these abuses, and campaign for change. Global Witness is an independent nonprofit that works with partners around the world in its fight for justice.

Investigative Dashboard
website: https://investigativedashboard.org

Investigative Dashboard helps journalists anywhere to trace people, companies, and assets across the globe. The Investigative Dashboard is operated by the Organized Crime and Corruption Reporting Project, a not-for-profit network of award-winning investigative reporting teams. Investigative Dashboard is supported by international partner networks and donors.

Organized Crime and Corruption Reporting Project
website: www.occrp.org

The Organized Crime and Corruption Reporting Project (OCCRP) is an investigative reporting platform formed by forty nonprofit investigative centers, scores of journalists, and several major regional news organizations around the globe. Their network is spread across Europe, Africa, Asia, and Latin America. The organizaions teamed up in 2006 to do transnational investigative reporting and promote technology-based approaches to exposing organized crime and corruption worldwide.

United States Department of Justice
950 Pennsylvania Avenue NW
Washington, DC 20530-0001
phone: (202) 514-2000
website: www.foia.gov

Since 1967, the Freedom of Information Act (FOIA) has provided the public with the right to request access to records from any federal agency. It is often described as the law that keeps citizens in the know about their government. Federal agencies are required to disclose any information requested under the FOIA unless it falls under one of nine exemptions which protect interests such as personal privacy, national security, and law enforcement. The FOIA also requires agencies to proactively post online certain categories of information, including frequently requested records. As Congress, the president, and the Supreme Court have all recognized, the FOIA is a vital part of the United States's democracy.

WikiLeaks
https://wikileaks.org

WikiLeaks is a multinational media organization and associated library. It was founded by its publisher, Julian Assange, in 2006. WikiLeaks specializes in the analysis and publication of large datasets of censored or otherwise restricted official materials involving war, spying, and corruption. It has so far published more than ten million documents and associated analyses.

Bibliography

Books

Floyd Abrams. *The Soul of the First Amendment*. New haven, CT: Yale University Press, 2017.

Julian Assange, Jacob Appelbaum, Andy Müller-Maguhn, and Jérémie Zimmermann. *Cypherpunks: Freedom and the Future of the Internet*. New York, NY: OR Books, 2016.

Charlie Beckett. *WikiLeaks: News in the Networked Era*. Cambridge, United Kingdom: Polity, 2012.

Benedetta Brevini, Arne Hintz, and Patrick McCurdy. *Beyond Wikileaks: Implications for the Future of Communications, Journalism and Society*. Basingstoke, UK: Palgrave Macmillan, 2013.

Christian Christensen. *WikiLeaks: From Popular Culture to Political Economy*. Los Angeles, CA: USC Annenberg Press, 2014.

Scott Christianson. *100 Documents that Changed the World: From Magna Carta to WikiLeaks*. London, UK: Batsford, 2015.

Daniel Domscheit-Berg. *Inside WikiLeaks*. New York, NY: Crown, 2011.

Edward Jay Epstein. *How America Lost its Secrets: Edward Snowden, the Man and the Theft*. New York, NY: Knopf, 2017.

Glenn Greenwald. *No Place to Hide: Edward Snowden, the NSA, and the U.S. Surveillance State*. New York, NY: Metropolitan Books, 2014.

Malcolm Nance. *The Plot to Hack America: How Putin's Cyberspies and WikiLeaks Tried to Steal the 2016 Election*. New York, NY: Skyhorse Publishing, 2016.

WikiLeaks and Julian Assange. *The WikiLeaks Files: The World According to US Empire*. New York, NY: Verso, 2015.

Periodicals and Internet Sources

Tony Cox, "Is WikiLeaks Release Brave or Unethical?" Talk of the Nation NPR, November 30, 2010. http://www.npr.org/2010/11/30/131699467/is-wikileaks-release-brave-or-unethical.

Emma Grey Ellis, "WikiLeaks has Officially Lost the Moral High Ground," *Wired*, July 27, 2016. https://www.wired.com/2016/07/wikileaks-officially-lost-moral-high-ground/.

Raffi Khatchadourian, "Julian Assange, A Man Without a Country," *New Yorker*, August, 21, 2017. https://www.newyorker.com/magazine/2017/08/21/julian-assange-a-man-without-a-country.

Kaj Larsen, "How WikiLeaks has Changed Today's Media," CNN, June10, 2011. http://www.cnn.com/2011/WORLD/europe/06/10/wikileaks.journalism/index.html.

Trevor Timm, "A WikiLeaks Prosecution Would Endanger the Future of US Journalism," *Guardian*, April 21, 2017. https://www.theguardian.com/commentisfree/2017/apr/21/wikileaks-prosecution-endanger-future-journalism.

Karl Vick, "WikiLeaks Is Getting Scarier Than the NSA," *Time*, August, 12, 2016. http://time.com/4450282/wikileaks-julian-assange-dnc-hack-criticism/.

Michael Youhana, "The Case for WikiLeaks as Legitimate Journalism," Mic, June 8, 2011. https://mic.com/articles/530/the-case-for-wikileaks-as-legitimate-journalism#.GLiTaocoN.

Eric Zorn, "When Media Publish WikiLeaks Documents: Legal, but Is It Ethical?" *Chicago Tribune*, July 28, 2016, http://www.chicagotribune.com/news/opinion/zorn/ct-wikileaks-dnc-emails-russia-media-ethics-zorn-perspec-0729-md-20160728-column.html.

Index